Peyton Place

Also by James Rosin*...

Philly Hoops: *The SPHAS and Warriors*

Rock, Rhythm & Blues

Philadelphia: *City of Music*

Route 66: *The Television Series*

Naked City: *The Television Series*

Wagon Train: *The Television Series*

Adventures in Paradise: *The Television Series*

Quincy, M.E.: *The Television Series*

The Invaders: *A Quinn Martin TV Series*

The Streets of San Francisco:
A Quinn Martin TV Series

*James Rosin's books are available on
www.**classictvseries**books.com
or by visiting amazon.com

Peyton Place
The Television Series

JAMES ROSIN

Published by THE AUTUMN ROAD COMPANY, Philadelphia, PA

Copyright © 2010 James Rosin
Revised 2012
All rights reserved.

No part of this book may be reproduced in any form or by any electronic or mechanical means including information storage and retrieval systems without permission in writing from the publisher, except by a reviewer who may quote brief passages in a review.

Design: Ronald Dorfman
www.RonaldDorfmanDesign.com

Printed by:
Lightning Press, Totowa, NJ
www.lightning-press.com

ISBN: 978-1-46750808-7

William Self (pictured in 1955 as producer of *Schlitz Playhouse of Stars*). As Vice President of 20th Century Fox Television in 1964, Self played an integral part in developing and bringing *Peyton Place* to network television. His selection and support of executive producer Paul Monash was decisive to the show's success.

*We are scaling the sheer face of television's Annapurna.
No one has ever scaled the east face before.
No one has ever tried. We will be the first and
I believe we will succeed. Where are the Sherpas?*

—Paul Monash, *March, 1965*

```
                    TWENTIETH CENTURY-FOX TELEVISION, INC.
                            INTER-OFFICE CORRESPONDENCE
                                                    DATE   August 2   66
TO:  WRITERS                                 FROM      PAUL MONASH
                 SUBJECT




             You will be pleased to know that,
             very largely through your brilliant
             work, PEYTON PLACE, in the last
             30-city Nielsens, ranked 1st, 2nd,
             and 3rd....or, if you like, 3rd,
             2nd, and 1st.



                                    P.M.

             PM/ld
```

Memo from executive producer Paul Monash to the writing staff of *Peyton Place*, August 2, 1966.

Contents

Acknowledgements .... *xi*
Author's Note .... *xiii*
About the Series 17

Photo Section
following page 65

Broadcast History 121
    Principal and Secondary Cast 121
Season One Summation 125
Season Two Summation 139
Season Three Summation 151
Season Four Summation 165
Season Five Summation 177
Sample Teleplay 183
Production Staff 193
The Daytime Series 197
The Two Network TV Movies 199
Biographies 203
End Notes 251
About the Author 253

Acknowledgements

I EXPRESS MY GRATITUDE to the following people who contributed to this book: David Canary, Everett Chambers, Michael Christian, Ruby Dee, Tom Del Ruth, John Erman, Michael Gleason, Lee Grant, Jeffrey Hayden, Robert Hogan, John Kerr, Irvin Kershner, Rita Lakin, Dorothy Malone, Ann Marcus, Ed Nelson, Tim O'Connor, Ryan O'Neal, Barbara Parkins, Ted Post, Del Reisman, William Self, Jack Senter, William Smithers, Elizabeth Walker, John Wilder, and Leigh Taylor-Young.

I also thank Marvin E. Livingston, Gary Girard and the *Peyton Place* fans for providing me with source information via Marvin's website devoted to the *Peyton Place* television series (Marvin1934.tripod.com); Ned Comstock of the USC Cinematic Arts Library, television historian Stephen Bowie, and Ed Hutson of Twentieth Century Fox.

Author's Note

THE STORYLINE SUMMATIONS for the five seasons are an overview of what were considered the most significant plot points. In reviewing 3,500 scenes in 514 episodes, the summary for each season could not include all of the nuances and interaction between the many characters. That is a book in itself. However, it does give emphasis to what was considered important and relevant.

Amidst the tone of church bells we were introduced to the continuing story of a small New England town unlike any other we had ever known before.

Peyton Place
About The Series

*P*EYTON PLACE DEBUTED September 15th, 1964 on the ABC Television Network. It first aired as two half-hour episodes every Tuesday and Thursday nights at 9:30 P.M. The show was television's first nighttime serial. The storylines were continuous with no reruns or summer hiatus, unlike any prime time network television series before or since. The production values were excellent, the writing was crisp, clever and literate, and the acting was honest and truthful.

The series would explore American morality and drift into occasional melodrama, while building a captivated audience that remained largely faithful for 514 episodes over the course of five seasons (1964–1969). At its peak, 60 million viewers followed the problems of the *Peyton Place* residents that they related to and found meaningful in their own lives.

Peyton Place was originally a best-selling novel by Grace Metalious about life in a small New England town. Published in 1956, the sensational content of the book offended some, intrigued others, and created controversy.

In 1957 Jerry Wald produced the feature film for Twentieth Century Fox with a cast that included Lana Turner, Lloyd Nolan, Diane Varsi, Lee Philips, Hope Lange, Betty Field, Arthur Kennedy, Russ Tamblyn, Terry Moore, David Nelson, Barry Coe, Mildred Dunnock, Leon Ames, and Lorne

Greene. The movie, directed by Mark Robson, was a huge box office success (although considered a laundered version of the book), and spawned a sequel four years later. *Return to Peyton Place* featured Jeff Chandler, Carol Lynley, Eleanor Parker, Robert Sterling, Mary Astor, Tuesday Weld, Luciana Paluzzi and Brett Halsey. The film was directed by Jose Ferrer with the title theme sung by Rosemary Clooney.

The video incarnation of *Peyton Place* first began when ABC program chief Leonard Goldenson saw the highly successful British nighttime soap opera *Coronation Street* during a trip to England in 1962. Upon his return to the U.S., Goldenson met with Twentieth Century Fox about producing something similar for American television. ABC was third behind the other two networks and Goldenson was determined to take a chance on something different. Fox has enjoyed an on-going relationship with ABC in producing hour-long dramatic series that included *Adventures in Paradise, Hong Kong, Follow the Sun* and *Bus Stop*.

WILLIAM SELF *(In charge of TV Production for Twentieth Century Fox 1962–1974)*

> When it came to my attention that Leonard Goldenson wanted to do a nighttime serial, the idea of doing *Peyton Place* became a possibility. I ran the 1957 film and afterward agreed with the potential of a series based on the movie. I had several executives under contract at that time including Paul Monash who was in charge of developing dramatic series. Paul was lukewarm about doing a soap opera and reluctant to get involved. However, I convinced him that this would be a unique project in prime time and he agreed to write the pilot and serve as executive producer.[1]

In the fall of 1963, a pilot was written by Monash and filmed by director Irvin Kershner.

IRVIN KERSHNER *(Director)*

We were casting in New York and I remember meeting a young girl who came into our meeting barefoot. This very gentle eighteen-year-old with flowing, golden hair was named Mia Farrow. (Her late father was movie director John Farrow, and her mother was actress Maureen O'Sullivan). She told me she had never done television before, yet there was something very special about her. I later cast Ryan O'Neal (who had been in a series called *Empire*) and Barbara Parkins, a beautiful Canadian-born actress (who had been in a dozen episodic TV shows). When we began filming, I recall Barbara's mother being on the set and protecting her from all the young men on the crew who were very interested in getting to know her daughter.[2]

ABC had some reservations about the pilot and asked Monash to submit an extended storyline for the first year of the series. Monash agreed but warned of possible changes. Once these changes began, the network became concerned and hired Irna Phillips, the renown creator/writer of daytime drama, as a creative consultant.

Monash and Phillips disagreed on many details, yet it was decided to make some alterations. The Cross family (major characters in the feature film and pilot) were dropped. Their family situation was deemed too sordid for network television. Michael Rossi who had been a high school principal became a doctor. The younger characters in the show were graduating from high school and wouldn't be spending much time there. Also, by making Rossi a doctor, it would bring him into the lives of various characters. Matthew Swain who had been an elderly doctor became the editor of *The Clarion* (the town newspaper), and ultimately served as narrator of the series.

Initially there was concern with regard to the title of the show. While it insured network and advertisers' attention, its content might scare off sponsorship. For a time the project was called *Eden Hill* and projected as a one-hour series, but reverted back to *Peyton Place*.

Because *Peyton Place* was a serial, many referred to it as a soap opera. Monash felt the term was pejorative. Instead, he preferred to call his project a television novel, the difference being the concept and quality of the stories which were more tightly packed. His show would have two or three stories interwoven like a feature, which allowed for character development. The series would retain the same basic characters at the start, but what happened to them was entirely different than what took place in the two feature films, and the book was never used as a reference.

The network had concerns about the moral tone of the series, but Monash had no interest in shocking his viewers. Instead he sought to create a show with strong situations and characters that would evoke interest, belief and sympathy. Monash felt if he made his audience feel the characters were real in the face of the problems that could face them, he would have a successful show.

JOHN WILDER *(Staff Writer 1965–1968)*

What made *Peyton Place* so unique was Paul's insistence that it had to be more than the nighttime soap opera envisioned by the network. For him and therefore all of us, it was always a novel. He had us looking to the likes of some of our greatest literary talents for many of our characters' actions and the conflicts they would encounter. There were no stereotypical characters from a daytime serial.[3]

TIM O'CONNOR *(Elliot Carson 1965–1968)*

Paul and his staff cleverly selected the characters and what they represented so that they appealed to the mass audience. They pushed at the norm of our culture and kept the series focused on things that were a little more ripe than what happened in the everyday family. The events and situations that occurred may not have wound up the way you expected them to within the confines of your own experience, yet that's what made *Peyton Place* so intriguing to its audience.[4]

RYAN O'NEAL *(Rodney Harrington 1964–1969)*

We were very fortunate to have momentum at the outset. The novel had created attention and there were two feature films that preceded us. We also had a terrific theme song that the producers were able to use from the original feature film, and there was some wonderful footage of New England locations that was incorporated into the show.[5]

EVERETT CHAMBERS *(Producer 1965–1969)*

The success of our series never relied on one star or gimmick. We had a huge cast of regulars. No other nighttime show could make that claim. We had the advantage of doing all facets of drama, melodrama and psychological drama when we chose to. We could go in multi-directions. Many notable actors were interested in working on *Peyton Place* because they got to grow in their characters with a huge audience.[6]

BARBARA PARKINS *(Betty Anderson 1964–1969)*

The television family at that time was always depicted in an *Ozzie and Harriet* type fashion where every family was nearly perfect or strived to be. The real conflicts, frustrations, and demons within the family structure were never explored. *Peyton Place* was the first television series to bring things out that were considered hush-hush and secretive. Families are highly complex and our show explored the complexities of teenagers, mother/daughter relationships, and family conflicts within a small town admosphere.[7]

Originally, *Peyton Place* featured a cast of twelve: Dorothy Malone (Constance MacKenzie), Ed Nelson (Doctor Michael Rossi), Warner Anderson (Matt Swain), Mia Farrow (Allison MacKenzie), Ryan O'Neal (Rodney Harrington), Barbara Parkins (Betty Anderson), Christopher Connelly (Norman Harrington), Paul Langton (Leslie Harrington), Kasey Rogers (Julie Anderson), Mary Anderson (Catherine Harrington), Henry Beckman (George Anderson), and Patricia Breslin (Laura Brooks).

Dorothy Malone was a former beauty contest winner from Texas. She had appeared in films since the late 1940s, and won an Academy Award (Best Supporting Actress) for her performance in the 1956 film *Written on the Wind*.

DOROTHY MALONE *(Constance MacKenzie 1964–1968)*

> Once I read the first three scripts, what stood out and appealed to me was the mother/daughter relationship and Constance's effort to protect Allison. Being the mother of two daughters in real life, I related to that very strongly, and during Mia's time on the show that was a very important part of the series.[8]

ED NELSON *(Dr. Michael Rossi 1964–1969)*

> Dorothy's character was originally supposed to be in real estate which would allow her to take the audience

to the other members of the cast. However, when I became the doctor, that would be my responsibility. So Constance became a bookstore owner.[9]

DOROTHY MALONE

Our show had a serious tone and Ed had a terrific sense of humor. He provided a much needed sense of relief while we were working.[8]

BARBARA PARKINS

When things got problematic or someone was down, the person who always brought joy to the show and kept things afloat was Ed Nelson. He was positive and upbeat. If someone had a problem, Ed would help them through it. He was this wonderful kind of "captain of the ship."[7]

DAVID CANARY *(Russ Gehring 1965)*

I was a twenty-something actor and new to television when I came on the show. I recall talking with Ed one day about how to play a particular scene. He said, "David, play everything 'grey' because most likely a week from now you'll be saying the exact opposite." While I never played anything grey, his point was well taken. Soap opera is mercurial in nature, opposed to everything else you do which has a beginning, middle and end, giving the actor a sense of where the character is going.[10]

ED NELSON

> I enjoyed becoming a physician although I didn't realize I would never cure most of my patients. I once asked Paul (Monash) if I could save one patient's life on the show rather than have them die. He replied, "saving people is boring," and even used me to write Catherine Harrington out of the show. As it turned out, my bedside manner was needed more than green scrubs and, although I was often in my office, it was not to deal with medical problems, but philosophical and moral issues.[9]

Paul Monash and company would generally probe the hidden motivations of their characters and use those motivations to create situations and advance them. However, Michael Rossi was one character Monash chose not to probe too deeply. This was alluded to in his character notes.

PAUL MONASH *(Executive Producer 1964–1969)*

> We should strive to make Rossi a little bigger-than-life. We should put behind him uncertainties, adorn him with positive attitudes, make him someone who does rather than someone who thinks. Like the skillful surgeon he is, Michael Rossi should cut to the heart of the matter. I believe the opportunity has risen to make Michael Rossi a series hero without in any way distorting his background.[11]

During the first season, the series focused on the secrets and scandals of the aforementioned characters. Constance and Allison MacKenzie were placed at the center of the story. Aside from conflicts Allison experienced with her over-protective mother, she becomes involved in a romantic triangle with Rodney Harrington and Betty Anderson. A definite contrast existed between Allison and Betty that provided for a broader audience appeal.

BARBARA PARKINS

> Betty was classified as a "bad girl." She liked to be provocative and experimental; kind of a wild child of that period. Allison was more introverted, wanting the comforts of a teenager and love in her life but not exploring it.[7]

Monash felt a concern that his characters not become involved in static situations, especially Allison MacKenzie, whom Monash felt was a very unique character.

PAUL MONASH *(from his character notes)*

> We are confronted by the imminence of Allison's womanhood. This could be underlined by the party given for (or which she gives for) her eighteenth birthday. Has she stepped over a threshold? A threshold of what? Basically, we must decide whether anything will happen to Allison and how it might happen in a way which would not destroy her utterly as that unique person in our series who manages to touch others and hopefully the audience. The dangers are these:
>   a) keeping Allison a Vestal Virgin; and
>   b) defiling the sanctuary.
>
>   In a very real sense, Allison has not yet been "awakened." In our first episodes, Prince Charming did kiss Sleeping Beauty (they may originate in two separate fairy tales but we do interweave in *Peyton Place*), and shimmers of apprehension begin to course through Constance. Now, I think that same Prince Charming [Rodney Harrington] is going to become the White Knight, safeguarding Allison. But Allison has been slumbering so long that the fires are banked. How can they be rekindled?[11]

At the same time, Monash voiced concern that Rodney Harrington, a very valuable character, not merely react to the events in the lives of other people.

PAUL MONASH *(from his character notes)*

We must provide him with an interesting life of his own, something which takes him beyond his current role of surrogate father to Norman and Lord Protector of Allison's virtues. It would be best if this story relates to the characters we already have. I believe that one more tributary story would cause our main stream to flood its banks.[11]

It remained important for Monash to keep his young characters well in the foreground. He considered them the most volatile, most tangible, and in some ways the most believable.

RICHARD DEROY *(Executive Script Consultant 1964–1968)*

When the show began shooting, we were finding our way. Some of our storylines tapped into something very fundamental with our audience. Young people are very easy to write about because they're facing their major choices, and our show was blessed by casting. Mia Farrow, Ryan O'Neal and Christopher Connelly were all perfect.[12]

LEE GRANT *(Stella Chernak 1965–1966)*

I was enchanted by the young actors on the show. Mia had an aura about her with her long, blonde, *Alice in Wonderland* hair. The innocence and naiveté that she registered was attractive and appealing to many people.

Barbara was very talented and a very pretty girl off-camera. However, on-screen she was exquisite.[13]

TED POST (*Director 1964–1969*)

Barbara had a warm grasp of Betty Anderson, captured the emotional needs of her character, and engaged the audience immediately. Mia had a very strong sense of truth and honesty on film. She was completely open with no hidden purpose, an unpretentious spirit that could do no wrong. Ryan possessed a vulnerability that heightened the emotional values of Rodney, and he also had a priceless sense of humor.[14]

BARBARA PARKINS

Someone often overlooked was Chris Connelly (Norman Harrington). He was a wonderful young actor with sort of a "Brando-esque" quality. Yet no one ever mentioned him. He was kind of invisible on the set. I would sometimes gaze at him and think he was so interesting-looking. Yet he always seemed to remain in Ryan's shadow.[7]

Ironically, Paul Monash created a powerful storyline for Norman Harrington at a point during season one when the series lacked hard drama. (He felt Chris Connelly would come into his own.) Monash deemed Norman a rebel who would act out in a direct way. His relationship with Rita Jacks (a working-class girl with a troubled past) involves him with her menacing ex-boyfriend who harasses and molests her. This builds to a confrontation where he inadvertently causes the death of Rita's ex-suitor.

The storyline was revised to involve older brother Rodney in a fight with Rita's former boyfriend (Joe Chernak), but

Norman remains a primary player, displaying fits of anger, jealousy, guilt, insecurity, and anguish in his relationship with Rita and encounters with Chernak. The story revision served a dual purpose. As a result of the confrontation on the wharf, Rodney is arrested, stands trial for murder, and this establishes a new set of conflicts for his character.

In the spring of 1964, Paul Monash was able to assemble a writing staff under executive script consultant Richard DeRoy that initially consisted of Robert J. Shaw, Theodore and Mathilde Ferro, Franklin Barton, Sonya Roberts and Richard Carr. Nina Laemmlie and Del Reisman joined the show as co-head writers during the first season and by the summer of 1965, a revised writing staff (under DeRoy, Laemmlie and Reisman) was assembled that mostly remained intact for over three years.

DEL REISMAN *(Associate Producer 1965–1969)*

> We were probably one of the first dramatic television series to have an in-house writing staff. Our core group consisted of Sonya Roberts, Michael Gleason, Carol Sobieski, John Wilder, Lionel Siegel, Jerry Ziegman, Peggy Shaw, Rita Lakin and later Ann Marcus.[15]

JOHN WILDER

> Carol (Sobieski), Jerry (Ziegman), Michael (Gleason) and I were all in our twenties when Paul (Monash) rolled the dice with us; and we all benefitted greatly from the knowledge of a man who was a master at his craft. The four of us referred to the experience as our renaissance workshop because we were writing for male and female characters ranging from children to grandparents; from an unschooled garage mechanic to an erudite multi-millionaire; from a salty tavern owner in

the wrong end of town to lawyers, doctors and journalists who were the pillars of the community.³

RITA LAKIN *(Staff Writer 1965–1966)*

Most of us were young and starting out. We all enjoyed what we did and got along very well. We worked in the Old Writer's Building on the Twentieth Century Fox lot which had a great deal of history. (I would look out my window and watch Doris Day play with her dogs on the lawn.)

We would be given an outline for an episode from Richard, Del, or Nina that described what took place in each scene. We would then write the dialog. Two of us would write a thirty-minute episode with each person doing one act which was basically fifteen pages. In a way, it was like a patch quilt, but it seemed to work well. We all had offices next to each other and each of us knew what everyone was doing. We were able to communicate all the time and make sure nothing was repeated.¹⁶

In story conferences, the writing staff would gather together with Paul Monash.

JOHN WILDER

There was a tremendous amount of creative energy in those meetings and everyone would chime in with their ideas. Yet it was Paul who could take all of what was discussed, sum it up and set the tone and pace. Dick, Nina and Del would plot it all out in a succession of episodes, yet all the final judgments and decisions were made by Paul.³

Monash proved to be the heart and soul of *Peyton Place*, yet he invited and encouraged creative contributions from the writers he had assembled. This was evident in a memo to his writers in March of 1965 in reference to his character and storyline notes.

PAUL MONASH

It is not accidental that these notes are being reproduced on paper with holes on the side. We should all look upon these as leaves in a loose-leaf notebook. From time to time, some of these pages will be eliminated, some will be amplified, and others will be introduced. I hope that each and every one of you feels free to suggest changes in our current storyline, and especially I request that you suggest new storylines. The more of these notes that spring from your fertile minds, the better *Peyton Place* will be, and the more we will enjoy working on it. I feel it is very important to maintain the method of forward invention which has given this series reality and vitality. So you'll find that while these notes define characters (with these definitions always subject to new insight) and suggest plot development, I am very much aware that you can help our understanding of the characters and find more dramatic plot development as we go. These notes are designed to help us all go forward hand-in-hand.[11]

JOHN WILDER

Paul's praise, encouragement and criticism when needed inspired a general feeling of camaraderie among the writing staff and garnered a kind of team spirit that had us all pulling for each other to "hit" the scenes we wrote "out of the park."[3]

Occasionally, there were differences of opinion between the writers and story editors about characters and what should actually take place.

MICHAEL GLEASON *(Staff Writer 1965–1968)*

I was given a scene to write between Sandy Webber (Lana Wood) and Martin Peyton (George Macready). Sandy was having an affair with Peyton's grandson Rodney (Ryan O'Neal). Peyton considered her "trash" and offers Sandy a huge amount of money to leave town. So she does. I felt the ending was flat and proposed that when Sandy is offered the money, she take it, but throw it back in Peyton's face.

Nina (Laemmlie) didn't like that idea. She felt it was time for the Webber character to make her exit, so she should take the money and go. However, Dick (DeRoy) and Del (Reisman) were in favor of what I suggested and my ending prevailed. I felt it was appropriate. Martin Peyton was this powerful man who always controlled everyone; so this ending provided an unexpected twist and gave the scene an added color.[17]

DEL REISMAN

It was Paul's idea to bring the character of Martin Peyton to life. He was the town patriarch, tycoon and had a connection to everyone and everything. If he didn't own it, he influenced the people that did. He manipulated lives like a puppet master. So we deliberately allowed a certain amount of mystery as to how much he controlled. No matter how few scenes he appeared in, it was important to have his presence. One of us came up with the idea of how to introduce him. He would be seated with his back to camera. We would see his arm hanging over one side and slowly we'd reveal him. It was an effort to intrigue a bit before we actually saw him. Paul disapproved of that idea and preferred Peyton to debut in a different way.[15]

In episode 133 (shown October 26, 1965) Peyton first appears in a confrontational scene with his former son-in-law. Leslie Harrington travels to Peyton's medical clinic in Boston to seek financial aid for Rodney's bail and legal defense. Leslie enters Peyton's suite unannounced. From his wheelchair, Peyton expresses his hatred for Leslie for the way he treated his daughter Catherine and for defiling her memory. In episode 151 (on December 6th) Peyton returns to *Peyton Place* for the murder trial of his grandson.

During season one Martin Peyton is an unseen presence with a debilitating illness. However, when he comes to life, we find he is not weakened emotionally and upon his arrival in Peyton Place his drive intensifies. His motivation, intention and conflict are outlined by Paul Monash in his 1965 character notes.

PAUL MONASH

Martin Peyton's drive is partly explained by the fact that his family gave its name to *Peyton Place*. And *Peyton Place* is the mill. And nothing must end. Yet something is ending. There is no Peyton left. There are two boys named Harrington. Martin Peyton is seeking the answer to two questions:

1) Which of the boys is in spirit, manner, and feeling a Peyton? 2) Which of the boys can eventually take over the running of the mill?

It is Martin Peyton's fervent hope that one of the boys (Rodney or Norman) will be both. But there exists several possibilities: 1) both may be Peytons; 2) neither may be a Peyton; 3) one may be a Peyton but not capable of growing into the management job; 4) the boy who is a Harrington rather than a Peyton may be the one who is capable… and so on. Knowing that his time on earth is measured, Martin Peyton must try to find the answer.[11]

As the series progressed, the story editors were plotting out about eight to ten weeks in advance.

DEL REISMAN

Sometimes we would have a full story episode that we would plot over several segments, intertwined with other happenings rather than isolate it for one episode. We had the freedom to do that and it proved to be very effective.[15]

Another asset of the series writing system was its flexibility. Generally, a thirty-minute show was based on a thirty page script. However, the story editors would not predict the page count of a scene as it was plotted out. So if an episode came out at forty-five pages, the last fifteen pages could become part of the next episode. This freedom to juggle scenes proved very helpful in terms of maintaining artistic quality and meeting schedule deadlines.

DEL REISMAN

On occasion we found that one writer was particularly skillful at writing for a specific character. So we would want that person to write the scenes for that character for a span of two to three episodes. The problem with that situation was screen credit. Most of the time, the credits listed the two writers for that episode, but in this case neither of them had written all of the scenes.

When the third writer saw they had not received screen credit, they got upset. So the agreed upon rule between the studio and Writers Guild was that the writing staff's names would appear a certain number of times within a six to eight week period. That seemed to appease all.[15]

All final shooting scripts were shot as written. Directors were not permitted to change so much as a word of dialog without Monash's personal approval.

JOHN WILDER

If any improvisational change was made by actors or directors who did not know what twists and turns were coming in ensuing episodes, it could mean costly re-shooting of the altered scenes.[3]

Story and character notes given by Monash to his writers were considered confidential and addressed in a Monash memo.

PAUL MONASH

Without making an espionage melodrama of this, I've numbered all the copies of these notes. You all understand the damage that can occur if these notes do receive anything but controlled distribution.

In particular, I do not wish members of the cast to become aware of the contents of these notes or even of their existence. When I am asked by members of the cast about story developments, my eyes glaze (and my knees buckle). The proper stance and expression will be demonstrated on request. I know you will penetrate my feeble cloud of humor and see the monument of seriousness in this.[11]

Scripts were also subject to network censorship which was

far more strict in the mid-1960s than it is today. ABC was very adamant about what was and was not allowed to be shown and heard.

BARBARA PARKINS

> When the show first aired, in bedroom scenes you had to have two single beds seven feet apart, and they would use a measuring tape to make sure. We were not allowed to sit on the bed separately or together. There was a highly puritanical attitude that existed then. Kisses and embraces were allowed but subdued. You never saw Rodney Harrington and Betty Anderson in a sexual situation. It came out in dialog that she was pregnant. Even then we received many letters saying "How dare you expose such a situation on television?" As the show evolved, you could be on a bed together, kind of sitting but not under the sheets. A lot was left to your imagination.[7]

LEIGH TAYLOR-YOUNG *(Rachel Welles 1966–1967)*

> We were carefully monitored by the network and not allowed to use words like "pregnant" and "sex." There were many instances where we had to find other ways to allude to things.[18]

Ted Post and Walter Doniger were the only two directors used for about the first ten months of filming.

WILLIAM SELF

> When I hired Ted and Walter, I told them they were being offered a difficult and demanding job. We had to

do two shows each week on a five-day shooting schedule. That meant filming a thirty-minute episode in two-and-a-half days. That was critical. I said, "If you can't, I'll understand, but then don't take the job." Both of them agreed to give it a try. They became very important to us because we never could have met that schedule without the help of these two directors. As the show progressed, we decided to use only Ted and Walter who alternated every two episodes. At that point, bringing in a new director who was unfamiliar with the characters and storyline seemed awkward. Eventually when we began to film three episodes weekly, we increased our staff.[1]

TIM O'CONNOR

Walter was more of a camera-oriented director. He would set up shots that were creative and interesting which he felt enhanced the storytelling. Yet they were complicated at times and you had to be very careful to be right on the spot.[4]

BARBARA PARKINS

What I appreciated about Walter was that he would encourage me at times to speak more with my eyes than with my words. He'd allow me that moment of silence where the look would sometimes express much more than the dialog.[7]

JOHN KERR

I felt Walter was more of a technician than an actor's director. I believe he felt the actors understood their characters and he relied on us to bring to the scene what was needed. If we didn't, he might make a comment.[19]

ED NELSON

Walter would challenge his crew with camera moves that coincided with specific actor positions. If we were one foot off the mark he'd shoot it again.[9]

WALTER DONIGER *(Director 1964–1968)*

During my four years on Peyton Place, I had what I thought was the finest crew in the business. If my script supervisor thought a take wasn't as good as it should be, she would tell me. And she was usually right. I had a best boy to the key grip who'd say, "Walter, you haven't given us a tough shot yet and we're getting bored." They liked difficult work and they'd do it fast. We would do from twelve to fifteen pages a day, shots with thirty moves, the crane, everything, and we'd be out by 5:00 or 5:30 P.M. when everyone worked 'til 7 or 8. I was known as a tough director. I wasn't tough in the sense of being a yeller or screamer. I just demanded performance from the crew. I expected everyone to do his job well and work a full day.[20]

Ted Post entertained a different perspective about the actors and what took place in the scenes.

LEIGH TAYLOR-YOUNG

Ted was warm and embracing, and I liked the safety of his kindness. It allowed the actor's purpose to come from within.[18]

ROBERT HOGAN *(Rev. Tom Winter 1968–1969)*

> Ted was interested in what was going on in the scene and making it the best it could be. It was like working in the theater. He also allowed me to come to dailies which was very helpful because at that point in my career, I hadn't done much film. So I got to see what works and what doesn't.[21]

TED POST

> Each scene in every episode we filmed was about something. There was a purpose to what each character was trying to achieve. My focus was to see that the actors knew what they were trying to accomplish and help them if needed. Fortunately, our group of actors were so skillful, they understood the subtext behind their lines and made that emotional connection with the audience. My camera angles were tailored to what the actor was doing, and came out of what the character's objective was. This would reinforce the mood and meaning of the scene.[14]

TIM O'CONNOR

> Both Ted and Walter were very good directors with different approaches, but they both wanted to flush out what was happening in each scene and account for what was going to happen.[4]

A third director who joined the series during the second season (succeeding John Newland) was Jeffrey Hayden.

JEFFREY HAYDEN *(Director 1965–1966)*

Peyton Place was one of the best experiences I had in my career as a director. The acting and writing was special. You were able to devote more attention to character. I directed a lot of segments that featured most of the young actors on the show, and they were all enthusiastic, loved their characters, and worked very hard.[22]

JOHN ERMAN *(Director 1967–1969)*

Peyton Place was a class act in terms of its production values and the creative people that were involved with the show. When you directed, it was like working with a stock company. You had the same players week after week who knew their characters, yet the dramas were continually unfolding and relationships were changing.

The actors weren't afraid to try new things that were emotionally big because that kept them vital. That was the real joy of doing the show. You were working with performers that knew what they were doing, and had a confidence because they knew they would have their job for a while.[23]

RYAN O'NEAL

After my first three months on the show, I didn't think I had a job. Through some clerical error they forgot to pick up my contract after twenty-six episodes. I thought that was it. I remember going around saying good-bye to everyone. Then they realized their mistake and came to me. At that point I was in a position to negotiate. So I asked for my own dressing room, a parking space on the lot with my name on it, and billing in the opening credits instead of at the back which went by quickly and nobody saw.[5]

Another distinct characteristic of the series was the frequent camera movement composed of dolly, crane and hand-held shots.

EVERETT CHAMBERS

Peyton Place was not shot like your traditional film TV series. It was shot like a live soap opera doing long master shots with lots of camera and actor movement. If you had a four-page scene, you'd do a four-page master and do a lot of your over-the-shoulder shots and close-ups all in the one master, then cover the rest of your dialog. It was a fluid way of shooting and all of our directors used that technique.[6]

TOM DEL RUTH *(Assistant Cameraman 1967)*

The tremendous amount of camera movement on the show was unique because most of what you saw in series television at that time were set shots. On *Peyton Place*, the camera was used in a gymnastic way to try and get as much page count in one shot, not allowing the camera to rest long enough where you would have to yell "Cut." In fact there began a thematic competition to see who could establish and stage the most exotic three or four-page scene without cutting. That was the most memorable experience for me to be moving around the way we did with such masterful configurations. It was not uncommon to have multiple dolly moves that could encompass anywhere from eight inches to as much as a hundred feet where the camera would dolly through rooms in the various sets introducing one character to another in a continuous flow of dialog without cutting. It was a difficult orchestration of the camera and the lighting to accomplish these shots but it kept up the pace of the show. The camera work gave the scenes an energy which they sometimes lacked, and in particular worked well on *Peyton Place* which was a continuous narrative without flashbacks or flash-forwards.[24]

When 20th Century Fox did the original feature film and the sequel, they shot much of the exteriors on location in New England. However, with the exception of local trips to Zuma Beach (which resembled the Northeast coastline) and Malibu Canyon (that created the illusion of countryside and sea) mostly all of the television series was filmed on the Fox lot in West Los Angeles due to cost concerns.

JACK SENTER *(Art Director)*

Toward the back of the main lot across from the commissary was a little park area that we decided to make into a town square. The gazebo and pillory marker on the grassy area was surrounded by a circular road that cars would drive around "360." We built a series of shops on the west side of the square which got natural light exposure most of the day. They included the Pharmacy, Antique Shop, Constance MacKenzie's Bookstore, Peyton Real Estate Office, Jewelry Shop, Peyton Professional Building (including the *Clarion* Newspaper office), and the Ship's Chandlery. The display windows in all of the shops were tilted to prevent reflections from the lighting. On the east side was the Colonial Inn (in reality the studio commissary) and later next to it the Police Station and Courthouse. At the corner was the Fire Department. The Interstate Bus Terminal was moved several times during the course of the series to accommodate the director. It wasn't a problem because it was always photographed head-on with no reverse shots.[25]

The greens department would bring in trees and shrubbery indicative of the spring, summer, and fall seasons. For winter scenes, gypsum that glittered like snow was used along with wind blowers to give the effect of a New England wintry day.

JACK SENTER

The gypsum was easier to put down than it was to take up. They used vacuums, brushes and water treatment to remove it and sometimes night crews were employed to change the square's appearance as we went from winter to spring.[25]

The town square and shops were shot at specific angles so as not to reveal the looming apartment and office buildings under construction north of the studio across Olympic Boulevard. This was the site of the up-and-coming Century City, once the studio's famed back lot. It was originally composed of 230 acres of sets used in countless films and TV series from the mid-1930s through the early 1960s.

Not all of the shop interiors were filmed on soundstages. Some were filmed on the square.

JACK SENTER

I extended the interior stage wall of the MacKenzie Bookstore about twenty feet so we could actually film inside when needed. That way on a reverse angle shot you could see people, cars, and activity outside in the square. You could shoot from either entrance and not feel you were on a studio set. That gave a more realistic setting without resorting to a process screen. It also saved time and allowed the directors to shoot out on the square and avoid moving inside to film on the stage.

When we shot in Dr. Rossi's office or Steven

Cord's office supposedly on the second floor of the Professional Building, we'd sometimes build a platform, bring in some side walls including a set wall with windows. That enabled the actors to look out onto the square below and see other characters that might be relevant to that scene.[25]

Around the corner from the northeast end of the *Peyton Place* Square past the Fire Department was the wharf area and boardwalk.

JACK SENTER

There we had a series of structures that included Ada Jack's Tavern, the Cider Barrel (which was also extended inside to show the wharf on reverse angles), the Shoreline Café, Boarding House and Shoreline Garage. Across the way was a schooner mounted on gimbles that allowed crew members to gently rock the structure when needed. Nearby was a loading chute for ice-fishing off the pier.[25]

RYAN O'NEAL

Alongside the bottom of the schooner were troughs of water with mirrors set up to cast reflections on camera and give the appearance of a boat in water.[5]

Interiors were shot on Stage 9 which housed a number of permanent sets at the outset, including the Harrington home, MacKenzie home, Anderson home, Norman and Rodney's room, the Clarion newspaper office, hospital corridor and Rossi's office. Other sets were constructed on Stages 3, 4, 7 and 12.

Because *Peyton Place* was a continuing drama, new

characters would appear and figure prominently in the plot for extended periods of time before making their exit.

JOHN KERR (John Fowler 1965–1966)

> I came onto the show toward the end of the first season as District Attorney John Fowler. What happened with a number of new characters that were introduced in the storyline was that they appeared in a kind of guest role for a specific number of shows; then the story might gradually develop around their character who became more prominent. That happened with me and I remained on *Peyton Place* for a year. I began as an attorney prosecuting Rodney Harrington, then the writers began to give me more personal issues to deal with apart from the trial.[19]

Other notable actors that played prominent roles during the course of season one included Kent Smith, Mariette Hartley, and Leslie Nielsen in a dual role of twin brothers.

Near the end of the first year, Lee Grant debuted as Stella Chernak and subsequently delivered an Emmy Award-winning performance.

LEE GRANT

> Mostly everyone else in *Peyton Place* were basically good people. Stella was a girl from the "other side of the tracks." Her father Gus was a malcontented watchman at the Peyton Mill, her younger brother Joe was always in trouble and ultimately died as a result of a fight with Rodney Harrington. Stella was a disturbed and unhappy character. It was an emotional role which suited me just fine as an actress. What was also nice about doing the show was that it was a welcoming set composed of

people who truly liked each other. That was very conducive to working.[13]

During the 1964–1965 season, *Peyton Place* became a well-established hit. The Tuesday night episode placed in the top twenty and the Thursday segment placed in the top ten. The viewing audience doubled in summer months as reruns of competing programs were no match for first-run episodes of *Peyton Place*. Some of those watching developed a very strong connection to the characters on the show.

LEE GRANT

There were people who couldn't separate themselves from what was going on in the storyline. What happened on the show was very real to them. One time I was buying shoes in Santa Monica. It was right about the time of my father's funeral on the show. A woman in the shoe store saw me and asked the salesman to approach me. He said, "The lady asked why you were in the store buying shoes. Wasn't today the day of your father's funeral?" I told the salesman to tell her I was buying shoes for the funeral and going there directly from the store.[13]

JOHN KERR

I was in Bullock's Department Store in Westwood, and a lady stood in front of me waiting to pay for something. All of a sudden she turned around with a menacing look and said, "Why are you so mean to Rodney?" And she meant it! Here I was being recognized for my conduct, not my face. It demonstrated how much the viewing audience was involved in the show.[19]

Due to the enormous popularity, ABC decided to telecast an additional segment. On June 25, 1965, Peyton Place began airing Tuesday, Thursday and Friday nights from 9:30-10:00 P.M. Once ABC informed Paul Monash they were ordering another weekly episode, the executive producer shared his thoughts and concerns with his writing staff.

PAUL MONASH

Much of the story material will be dictated by the demands of our producing three half-hours a week on a fifty-two-week basis. This affects story material, mainly because it affects our use of cast.

For your information we will be basing our shooting schedule on the availability of cast. In order to prevent members of the cast being required in scenes being shot simultaneously, we must add running characters. In so doing we will be adding storylines. We will be faced with two choices: we can tell multiple stories within each episode, or we can try to organize our episodes around the cores of one or two stories, much as we do now.

There are dangers in each choice. We might slice our life too thin and lose impact; and we might also find our audience is not watching all our episodes each week and become confused unless we try to depict as much of *Peyton Place* in every half hour.

At this moment, I am not completely sure which path we should follow. This is one of the reasons why I am pressing for the completion of as many first draft scripts as possible. I feel that with a stockpile of first drafts, we will have a chance to organize our material and I think the choice will be made for us by the material itself.[11]

EVERETT CHAMBERS

Once we had a shooting script, doing three shows a week was not difficult from a production standpoint. After it was organized the storylines, cast and sets were the same. The important thing was to coordinate who and what sets were available. So you'd have one director do two episodes in five days and a second director would do his in three, scheduled according to how the cast and sets would dovetail with the other unit doing two episodes.[6]

TIM O'CONNOR

If we were in one location, we'd shoot all the scenes from two different episodes that took place in that location. So you had to be very familiar with each script and what happened from one segment to the next as your attitude and behavior might have totally changed. When we began doing three shows a week, the actors had even more responsibility. So everyone in the cast took extra care to monitor themselves with what they had to do and what was happening. We often worked all day and well into the night. It was very demanding, yet it created a very close-knit connection between the actors and spurred professional relationships.[4]

BARBARA PARKINS

Shooting three shows a week was harder work but we were all so excited and in love with this television series that we would have done anything with our actor energies to keep it flowing and maintain its popularity.[7]

Filming began every weekday morning about 8:00 A.M.

ED NELSON

The crew, the gaffers (who handled everything electric), the grips (who took care of the sets and gear), the camera crew, including the cinematographer, and the sound crew were often on the set an hour before the cast began arriving. The director and assistant director also showed early. After a cast call the director would ask for a run-through which established where the characters would start and how they would move around the set in accordance with the script's actions or character's attitude. The director made suggestions, the electricians lit the set, and soundmen placed the microphones in strategic locations, while actors did a final check with make-up, hair and wardrobe people. If there was enough time, we ran through the lines. When the technicians were ready, a final rehearsal was called. We took our places and did the scene as if it were final filming. After this, the crew might make final technical changes and the director might recommend performance adjustments to a cast member. Then we'd shoot the scene.[9]

Once ABC expanded *Peyton Place* to three nights, the network considered doing a spinoff series tentatively titled *The Girl from Peyton Place*, starring Barbara Parkins.

BARBARA PARKINS

The Betty Anderson character became so popular that the network came up with the idea to do a series where my character leaves *Peyton Place* and goes to New York. However, it didn't come to fruition.[7]

[It was theorized that the poor ratings for the third episode discouraged the network from developing a spinoff show.]

As the series filmed for the fall season in the summer of

1965, a crisis occurred which centered around Mia Farrow. Allison MacKenzie was a significant character and Farrow enjoyed a huge following. Attention seemed riveted on the twenty-year-old actress the moment she first appeared on the show. At the time, Farrow was dating Frank Sinatra who was filming *Von Ryan's Express* at Fox.

JEFFREY HAYDEN

> One day during shooting, Mia mentioned that she and Frank (Sinatra) would be going to an important engagement that evening. I reminded her that she was in the first shot the following morning and it was a big day for her. I had a lot of pages to get done and asked that she please not allow Frank to keep her out too late. "Kindly get home at a reasonable hour and get up on time and be here." The next morning, I'm walking through the set about 7 A.M. and Mia is nowhere to be found. My first shot is at 8 A.M. and still no Mia. So I begin shooting inserts and keep going until about 10:00. At 10:30 Mia arrives looking tired and haggard. She apologizes and explains that Frank insisted they go here and there, and no one would take her home. I said, "Mia, after the talk we had last night, you come in here over three hours late and tell me you're sorry? When are you going to grow up and become your own person?" She stood there teary-eyed, so sorry she couldn't say a word, then turned and walked away. I continued shooting another insert while she was at the makeup table. About five minutes later Mia approached me and in her hand was a clump of that long, beautiful hair that she had just cut off. She held it right up to my face and said, "No more little girl, Jeff." I thought to myself, "Wow." We've got to match yesterday's shot and I'm in a quandary. I immediately called Everett (Chambers) and explained what happened.[22]

EVERETT CHAMBERS

When I got down to the make-up department, Mia was sitting in the chair and the first thing I said to the hair stylist was "Get that hair back on her." Unfortunately, it was all over the floor.[6]

Once Chambers informed Paul Monash, the executive producer huddled with his head writers.

JEFFREY HAYDEN

A short time later, Everett called me on the set and told me he instructed the grips to put together three flats to make up a hospital room with a bed, and to put Mia in the bed. Her head would be wrapped in a bandage. The set was constructed and about thirty minutes later, a two to three page scene arrived that explained Allison MacKenzie was the victim of a hit-and-run.[22]

ED NELSON

When I arrived on the set, the impact of what Mia had done was staggering. So I decided to reduce the tension. I went over to see Ben Nye, Fox's make-up genius and he made me bald as a hen within ten minutes. I went back to the stage and I looked ridiculous. The cast and crew had a great laugh. So did Mia who crawled into bed with her chopped hair and bald physician at her bedside. We actually shot an ad-lib scene.[9]

RYAN O'NEAL

Mia's long flowing hair set a trend with teenage America. When she cut it, it made headlines in every newspaper. Then the studio brought in Vidal Sassoon to spruce it up and Mia's new hairstyle set another trend.[5]

Rumors abound as to why Mia Farrow cut her golden tresses. The truth was Farrow was an "unpretentious spirit" and, despite her celebrity status, never concerned with hairstyle and make-up. Her aversion to vanity combined with increasing public/media accolades about her hair made her wary. That morning as she waited impatiently to get her hair styled, bored with the situation and perhaps the show, she reached for a nearby scissors and cut her hair to within an inch in length. Shortly afterward, in August of 1965, Farrow was reluctantly permitted by the studio to take a four-week hiatus while she went on a New England yacht trip with Frank Sinatra.

MICHAEL GLEASON

> We were able to counteract Mia's absence by having her remain in a coma. There were occasional long shots of Allison in her hospital bed using a "double," combined with additional shots with the angle on Constance or Elliot at her bedside.[17]

More upheaval occurred in the MacKenzie-Carson household not long after Farrow's return to Peyton Place. Dorothy Malone was stricken by a serious illness on September 24, 1965. Blood clots were discovered in Malone's lungs and a rare operation was performed to save her life. Actress Lola Albright replaced Malone until the Academy Award-winning actress retuned to her role on November 19.

The murder trial of Rodney Harrington provided the focus for most of the first half of season two, followed by a new storyline centered around Ann Howard (Susan Oliver) out to resolve a traumatic childhood incident.

Allison MacKenzie recovers but is a confused and trouble young lady from then on. Her discovery of Ann Howard's body at the base of the cliffs pushes her over the edge. On August 29,

1966 (in episode 263) a disoriented Allison is last seen walking down the road north of the Shoreline Garage as the episode ends.

Six weels before, Mia Farrow had married Frank Sinatra and at his urging left the series. Farrow was content to spend time with her new husband and didn't work for eight months.

Paul Monash and his writers were unsure about Farrow's possible return, so Allison's disappearance was preferable to her being killed off.

Allison MacKenzie would remain in the consciousness of the writers and viewers for season three, as the show debuted in color. On October 12, 1966 (in episode 277), a replacement character was introduced with a link to Allison. Rachel Welles, a mysterious girl in her late teens, is found with Allison's bracelet sustaining a continued concern and curiosity as to her whereabouts. Chosen to play Welles was Leigh Taylor-Young, a New York actress fresh off the Broadway stage who had never worked before a camera.

LEIGH TAYLOR-YOUNG *(Rachel Welles 1966-1967)*

> I really wasn't interested in doing television at the time. I was living in New York and through some wonderful connections I had very good and well-known agents (Stark Hesseltine and Leo Bookman), and was working on Broadway. I loved being on stage and found it deeply inspiring. I had never been a big television viewer and had not even seen *Peyton Place* or realized how successful it was.[18]

After contracting pneumonia during a harsh New York winter, Taylor-Young sought the warmth and sunshine of California to recuperate. An affiliate of her New York agent arranged for her to meet Paul Monash and Everett Chambers. Ironically, Taylor-Young had previously met Monash during a mass casting call for *Peyton Place* in New York. The California meeting proved to be entirely different. Taylor-Young was offered a screen test and seven year contract. Barely twenty-one when offered the role, Taylor-Young opted to return to New York to continue her passion for the theater. Her mother convinced her otherwise.

LEIGH TAYLOR-YOUNG

> I saw television as pure entertainment, unlike the theater. Yet my mother convinced me that I could channel this inner idealism that I possessed into my work on *Peyton Place*, not in a diminished way but in a different fashion.[18]

Taylor-Young's screen test could have proved daunting for an actress who had never set foot on a soundstage, but Taylor-Young was theater-trained and prepared. Jeffrey Hayden directed the test which consisted of a scene from *The Glass Menagerie*. However, Taylor-Young was unaware of the excitement and curiosity among the actors on the show regarding her.

LEIGH TAYLOR-YOUNG

> When we did the test, all of the cast from the show lined up in a semi-circle behind the camera. So not only was I dealing with the first time of a camera dollying in on me while doing the scene, but with all of the actors in my sight line. However, I remained focused.[18]

Once cast in the role of Rachel Welles, the challenge for Taylor-Young was understanding acting in terms of the mechanics of film.

LEIGH TAYLOR-YOUNG

In the theater you have time and space to go deeply into a character. In television you work very fast and often without continuity. Sometimes you'd shoot the end of an episode on Monday and the beginning on Wednesday, without the benefit of filming in sequence. That's the nature of the medium. However, I was very taken with how well the show was written and I relished the role of Rachel. I understood her nature and innocence. She was abused to the degree that her need for love and attachment to the Carson family was so great, she would ultimately take on the persona of Allison.[18]

Prior to Rachel Welles' arrival, at the outset of the series' third year, a baby boy named Matthew is born to Constance and Elliot Carson (September 19, 1966, episode 270). That helps to fill the void left by their missing daughter.

Before Allison's disappearance, Paul Monash had toyed with the idea of Constance becoming pregnant, a later-in-life pregnancy for Constance and Elliot awaiting their legitimate off-spring. Monash outlined his reasons in his notes on the Carson family.

PAUL MONASH

In television, audiences 1) seem to wait for babies to be born—as in the "Lucy" show some years ago. 2) They seem to like babies when they are born. 3) It creates areas for Allison as well as her parents, areas of love and conflict. 4) It can involve medical complications, if we will. 5) Whatever might threaten their marriage from that outside source will post a greater threat if new life is coming into their home. I must confess also to a feeling that a marriage without children tends to become an arid arrangement usually involving dogs, cats and armadillos, and I therefore feel that Constance and Elliot will become wearisome if we try to play them as a romantic couple in our little town.[11]

For season three (1966–1967) ABC decided to eliminate the third chapter and go back to airing *Peyton Place* twice weekly.

WILLIAM SELF

The ratings for the third installment were not what the network expected and didn't justify continuing. I believe a lot of the viewing audience weren't willing to remain home three nights a week and make that commitment, especially on a Friday night.[1]

MICHAEL GLEASON

My mother-in-law was a big fan of the series, but when it went to three-a-week, said, "I don't have that kind of time." Because it was a serial, she not only skipped the third episode but didn't watch the first or second either. In trying to capitalize on the show's success, the network hurt the series ratings; and from then on our audience began to decline.[17]

Although the show resumed airing twice weekly, the production schedule of shooting three segments each week remained.

EVERETT CHAMBERS

When I came on the show they were always "on the wire" to get on the air. The actors never had vacations or time off unless someone was written out of the storyline so they could go off and do something. I preferred to continue doing three shows a week (even though we only aired two) because it enabled us to get much needed hiatus time. This way we were about twenty episodes and ten weeks ahead of air time.[6]

ROBERT HOGAN

Everett Chambers was well organized, hands-on, and made sure everything was carried out smoothly. He was also very supportive of the actors. Whenever he came on the set you never felt you were being judged or scrutinized. He always made you feel that you were part of the team.[21]

During the latter part of season three, in mid-June of 1967, actor George Macready (who portrayed Martin Peyton) took ill and was temporarily replaced by Wilfred Hyde-White. During Macready's convalescence, John Wilder (who wrote many of Martin Peyton's scenes) wrote Macready a letter of concern and tribute:

> Dear George:
>
> I greatly appreciate the style and mannerisms you bring to your concept of Martin Peyton. Out of respect for your creativity on the soundstage, I always make a special effort to assist at this and in scenes which involve you. I derive the same kind of joy in selecting the precise language used by our master manipulator that you convey in carrying out the actions of the plot.
>
> Each line I work out is designed (to the best of my ability) to fit the particular rhythms of delivery that you bring to this particular characterization. I even maintain a special file for words that I consider to be in Martin Peyton's domain alone as far as this show is concerned.

This morning I recognized a special challenge as I prepare to bring Betty and Peyton into conflict. Can I write Martin Peyton's dialog when I have just learned that Martin Peyton will not be delivering it? I hope to. I also hope Wilfred Hyde-White, a talented man too, will be able to reflect something close to that brand of wit, sensitivity and cynicism that you breathed into our white-haired patriarch.

I hope more than anything, however, that your health rallies rapidly.

It was distressing to hear of the illness and I for one—while urging you to make sure you are fully rested before you return—must confess I shall be pressed into doing some acting myself in your absence, pretending your unique approach and delivery will greet the lines I commit to paper.

My sincerest wishes for a prompt and permanent recovery.

Respectfully,
John Wilder
Old Writers Building

Wilder's letter prompted a response from Macready:

Dear John:

Your episode (which recently aired) is by far the best of all the episodes and gave my recovery a real boost. I was feeling a bit sorry for myself (I guess those who have never been sick before are inclined to) and your wonderful letter has cured that. I am off cigarettes, compensating by eating, so if you are considering writing a picture about the life of Fatty Arbuckle, please consider me for the role.

Sincerely,
George Macready

In the summer of 1967, as the series approached its fourth season and Rachel Welles made her exit, two new characters were introduced. Gena Rowlands debuted as Adrienne Van Leyden (on July 24 in episode 355), a beautiful woman brought to *Peyton Place* to undermine the marriage of Betty and Steve Cord. On August 21, (in episode 363) Dan Duryea appeared as con man Eddie Jacks (Rita's estranged father) who returns to town after walking out on his family many years before.

Four months into season four (in episode 402), Joyce Jillson was introduced as Jill Smith, a young woman who claims that Allison is the real mother of her baby; and a month later (on February 22, episode 411), newcomer Michael Christian debuted as Joe Rossi (Michael's younger brother) on the run from a criminal incident in New York.

MICHAEL CHRISTIAN *(Joe Rossi 1968)*

I auditioned for Paul Monash and Everett Chambers and did a scene from *On the Waterfront*. Fortunately, I had director George Cukor (a friend) sit in on one of my final rehearsals to make sure I was using all of myself and my traits as the character and not emulating Marlon Brando who did the film role. At one point when we did the audition, the other actor (Hagen Smith) who played my brother, shoved the gun so hard into my chest, it jammed underneath my throat and brought tears to my eyes. However, I used that in the scene. I sat there stunned and it really sold what we did. I picked that scene because like Joe Rossi, the character of Terry Malloy was a boxer and it was a scene between two brothers. The audition led to a great role on a Fox series *Felony Squad*, a thirty-minute police drama that starred Howard Duff, Dennis Cole, and Ben Alexander. Once Paul Monash saw the dailies, he cast me as Joe Rossi and I was on the show for a year.[26]

Also introduced (in episodes 419 and 421) were conflicted minister Tom Winter (Robert Hogan) and his troubled wife Susan Winter (Diana Hyland). In late May, 1968 (during the eighth month of season four) the characters of Constance and Elliot Carson (Dorothy Malone and Tim O'Connor) departed *Peyton Place*. Two new characters were introduced: recent divorcee Marsha Russell (Barbara Rush) and her troubled teenage daughter Carolyn (Elizabeth Walker). The Russells subsequently rented the Carson home for the summer. As *Peyton Place* rolled into its fifth year (1968–1969) the network decided to introduce more youth and relevance.

EVERETT CHAMBERS

After four years and over 460 episodes, our ratings began to wane. It was decided that we should shift gears and become more contemporary and youthful. There were riots, demonstrations, protests, and dissatisfaction going on in this country and it was time to catch up.[6]

It was decided integration would come to *Peyton Place*. An Afro-American neurosurgeon would first appear in July of 1968, and we would meet the remainder of his family sometime in the fall. Dr. Harry Miles (Percy Rodriguez) would be less of a doctor and more of a husband to his wife Alma (Ruby Dee) and father to their teenage son Lew (Glynn Turman). It was Paul Monash's idea to explore their characters. Certain prejudices would be displayed, especially when Lew Miles would become involved with Carolyn Russell, a white teenager. The integration of the Afro-American family in 1960s television was done gingerly and many felt there needed to be a dramatic breakthrough.

RUBY DEE *(Alma Miles 1968–1969)*

> From the beginning, the networks and artistic TV community approached inclusion of Afro-American storylines with timidity. For many years, the absence of black producers, writers and directors existed and stereotypical characters prevailed almost exclusively. However, introducing or suggesting an interracial relationship between my son on the show and Carolyn Russell was jumping too fast into the heat of controversy. That kind of situation was too personal and not part of a storyline that the general viewing audience was ready to accept or to identify with at the time.[27]

When a studio press release announced that the son of the new Miles family would have a relationship with a white female character on the show, an adverse reaction occurred. Adding fuel to the fire was an interview with actress Elizabeth Walker.

ELIZABETH WALKER *(Carolyn Russell 1968–1969)*

> Paul Monash came to New York and offered me the role of the American tragedy; a torrid teenage interracial affair resulting in pregnancy. I was doing a very dramatic play at the time and so it appealed to me and I went for it. I had no idea what I was letting myself in for, until a friend's father interviewed me for his very popular magazine. Unbeknownst to me, the article exposed the upcoming storyline. The result was I (in addition to the producers) received a lot of hate mail, and the southern stations threatened to stop airing the show. I was thrown at the time, but relieved when the producers eventually scrapped the idea. I was in no position or condition to handle that kind of tremendous controversy. Nor was my family.[28]

EVERETT CHAMBERS

I remember getting a letter from someone threatening to "nail me to my garage door." That reaction along with the volume of negative mail we received concerned me and I voiced those concerns to Paul. I also felt the whole Miles family scenario was coming from a white person's point of view with white writers and directors, and it didn't feel genuine. I suggested bringing in a black psychologist as a consultant and hiring some black writers. I found a black psychiatrist who reinforced the network's opposition to the idea of an interracial affair between the two teens. We also met with Ruby (Dee) and her husband Ossie Davis who both wanted to get out of a white fantasy and get into something true.[6]

DEL REISMAN

A great deal of thought went into the placing of the Miles family into the show because it was serial storytelling. We introduced Harry Miles initially. He first appeared in a brief scene with Michael Rossi and over the next eight weeks he appeared in more relevant scenes as we developed his character. In that way, the audience got to know him and sensed that he would become important. Then one day we followed him home and met his family. We wanted Harry, his wife Alma and his son Lewis to be dimensional characters and care was given to avoid clichéd behavior. Although we considered ourselves socially aware, we were still white people writing about a black family. Yet we made a sincere effort to give these characters the same dignity and equality that we gave to the other characters on the show.[15]

RUBY DEE

Despite the well-intentioned effort of the writers, there needed to be an honest look at the dynamics of racism and relevant circumstances. For example, the mistreatment of people who didn't deserve it. Harry Miles was an important neurosurgeon. Being a black doctor, what was his interaction with the other doctors and nurses? What about the attitude of patients who came to see him? What about the neighborhood where the Miles family lived? How were they accepted? The series missed the opportunity to dig deeper and be more visceral, to create conflicts that would tend to break down barriers between the races and create a more mature understanding and appreciation of each other, despite the difference in their backgrounds.[27]

ANN MARCUS *(Staff Writer 1967–1969)*

I remember writing a memo to Paul Monash because I didn't feel the Miles family portrayed on our show was your typical black family. They were somewhat segregated, contained, and not racially integrated in the other storylines. Paul was complimentary and praised my point of view but nothing came of it. (We were on at night and restricted by the network as to what direction we could go in.) Instead we developed a storyline where Rodney Harrington has a motorcycle accident which involved the Harry Miles character because he would have to operate.[29]

JOHN ERMAN

I thought that the Miles family storyline was "whitewashed," and I remember how uncomfortable Ruby was with the depiction. But you have to remember, at the time it was a daring thing to do; to have an Afro-American family on a show like *Peyton Place* which was really like *Our Town*. It was a complicated situation and I think everyone involved had to compromise.[23]

RYAN O'NEAL

Peyton Place was a somewhat insulated community. The show never really got into political, religious, or racial controversy. It was a series about people and their personal problems. That wasn't going to change.[5]

During the 1968–1969 season, the Monday night edition of *Peyton Place* was on opposite *Laugh-In* which was fresh, funny and a huge hit. It trounced *Peyton Place* in the ratings which affected the Wednesday night installment as well. People who watched *Laugh-In* on Monday night were less likely to watch the Wednesday night episode of *Peyton Place*.

DEL REISMAN

Our ratings decline brought social implications as well. A number of prominent blacks felt the American public was rejecting the concept of integrating a black family into a predominantly white television drama, and weren't ready for their appearance on primetime TV.[15]

EVERETT CHAMBERS

I don't believe the Miles family had anything to do with the drop in ratings. Five years of *Peyton Place* which aired 514 episodes were equivalent to 17 years of a regular series that aired once a week, because we never went into reruns. So eventually it wore out like everything else. That was to be expected. We were also on at an earlier time during our final season and that might have been a miscalculation. At 8:30 the audience was predominantly kids and *Peyton Place* was not a kid's show.[6]

By the time *Peyton Place* reached the end of its five year run on June 2, 1969, about 1,574,750 feet of film had taken the absorbing story of all the residents of *Peyton Place* into millions of viewers' homes. The cast was one of the largest ever assembled for a television series. Over seventy-five actors played important roles and over 8,000 checks were issued to bit players and extras. Thirty-four writers turned out scripts since the series began filming on June 8, 1964.

LEIGH TAYLOR-YOUNG

If you look back at the sixties with all that transpired in terms of assassinations, the Vietnam War, protests, and the spiritual movement, *Peyton Place* was a new concept. It touched off that spark of consciousness that wanted things brought out of the shadows where we could objectify and look at human behavior and be utterly fascinated by it.[18]

TED POST

There was an identification for the parent and the young person on *Peyton Place*. The young characters all struggled to find meaning in their lives while trying to overcome the burden of their parents' guilt and fears. The young and old of *Peyton Place* shared love, loneliness, and a continuing quest to communicate those feelings to those they cared about. Their moments of recognition and understanding resonated in the lives of the millions of people watching.[14]

The *Peyton Place* cast during filming of the original pilot in October, 1963. Pictured (left to right) are Mary Anderson (Catherine Peyton Harrington), Minnette King (Nellie Cross), Stephanie Lynn (Joannie Cross), Gyl Roland (Selena Cross), James Anderson (Lucas Cross), Kasey Rogers (Julie Anderson), Barbara Parkins (Betty Anderson), Ryan O'Neal (Rodney Harrington), Jon Lormer (rear, Corey), Ed Nelson (Michael Rossi), Dorothy Malone (Constance MacKenzie), Mia Farrow (Allison MacKenzie), Paul Langton (Leslie Harrington), Warner Anderson (Dr. Matthew Swain), and Sarah Selby (Elsie Thornton).

The Cross family was dropped from the cast prior to the series debut. Their storyline, which involved incest, was deemed unsuitable for network television. In addition, the characters of Corey and Elsie Thornton were not continued. However, actor Jon Lormer, did return as Judge Chester in the third season.

Allison MacKenzie (Mia Farrow) and Constance MacKenzie (Dorothy Malone). Their mother-daughter relationship was at the center of the storyline in the fall of 1964.

Dr. Michael Rossi (Ed Nelson) had a significant presence from the show's start to finish. Originally the character of Michael Rossi was a high school principal, but became a physician when the television series debuted.

Matt Swain (Warner Anderson) was editor of the *Clarion* (the town newspaper) confidant of Constance MacKenzie and a friend to those in need. He left the series at the end of the first season but remained as narrator at the opening, discussing a specific character and/or event.

Norman Harrington (Christopher Connelly) and Rodney Harrington (Ryan O'Neal) were caring brothers despite their differing perspectives.

Betty Anderson (Barbara Parkins) was among the few characters who remained with the series from beginning to end. Parkins was later picked by famed photographer Patrick Lichfield to be included in his 1983 book *The Most Beautiful Women*.

Attention was riveted on Mia Farrow the moment she appeared on screen as Allison MacKenzie. The innocence and naivete she registered appealed to many viewers.

A stark contrast existed between blonde, virtuous Allison MacKenzie (Mia Farrow), and dark-haired siren Betty Anderson (Barbara Parkins). Their conflicts involving female sexuality intrigued and captured an enormous viewing audience.

Leslie Harrington (Paul Langton) was a somewhat ruthless man with a weakness for his children. Despite this, he was frequently at odds with son Norman (Christopher Connelly).

Once the Cross family characters were dropped from the show an alternative storyline led to the pregnancy and miscarriage of Betty Anderson (Barbara Parkins).

Julie Anderson's (Kasey Rogers) affair with her employer, Leslie Harrington, was instrumental in the break-up of daughter, Betty (Barbara Parkins) and Rodney Harrington (Ryan O'Neal).

Dr. Robert Morton (Kent Smith), the Harrington family's personal physician, at first disapproves of Michael Rossi, but later becomes his ally and colleague. (Smith's wife in the series was portrayed by real-life wife actress Edith Atwater.)

Elliot Carson (Tim O'Connor) joined the series midway through season one. After he was revealed to be Allison's father, Carson married Constance MacKenzie and ultimately became editor of the *Clarion* newspaper.

Originally, the network wanted the character of Elliot Carson to be killed off and Constance MacKenzie to stand trial for his murder. Executive producer Paul Monash felt it too early to introduce melodrama into the storyline and refused. He won support from studio executive William Self and eventually the network accepted their position.

Rita Jacks (Patricia Morrow) first appeared during season one as a person from "the wrong side of the tracks" to whom Norman Harrington (Christopher Connelly) became attracted. They later married and she became an important character in the series.

Said Barbara Parkins: "When the show first aired, in bedroom scenes you had to have two single beds, seven feet apart. They used a measuring tape to make sure."

Dr. Claire Morton (Mariette Hartley) returns to *Peyton Place* planning to divorce husband Dr. Vincent Markham during season one, yet returns with him to Peru after a brief stay.

Dr. Vincent Markham (Leslie Nielsen) suffers from a rare blood disease but returns to South America to supervise a humanitarian project. (Nielsen also played twin brother Kenneth, a wealthy industrialist from Philadelphia).

The Schuster family: David (William Smithers), Doris (Gail Kobe) and daughter Kim (Kimberly Beck). Soon after David takes over as manager of the Peyton Mill, Kim becomes a key witness in the Rodney Harrington murder trial.

Don Quine (Joe Chernak) and Lee Grant (sister Stella Chernak) share a humorous moment on the set in the summer of 1965. Grant won a 1966 Best Actress Emmy Award for her performance in the series.

Marian Fowler (Joan Blackman) wonders how long she can keep her secret from husband John Fowler (John Kerr) during season two in the fall of 1965.

Veteran character actor Frank Ferguson appeared as kind and supportive Eli Carson who owned the Ship's Chandlery (later a general store). As Elliot Carson's father, Allison's grandfather and at one point Norman Harrington's employer, he was always somewhat involved in the lives of the other *Peyton Place* characters.

Physical therapist Russ Gehring (David Canary) works to rehabilitate Allison MacKenzie (Mia Farrow) the victim of a hit-and-run accident. When Russ feels Allison has become spoiled and lazy, he pushes her to make progress. Allison reacts by cutting her hair in defiance. This was how Farrow's hair cutting incident off-camera was explained in the storyline.

Tavern owner Ada Jacks (Evelyn Scott) was privy to much of the undercurrent in *Peyton Place* and involved with daughter Rita's conflicts and health issues.

Hannah Cord (Ruth Warrick) and Martin Peyton (George Macready) arrive in *Peyton Place* for the trial of his grandson Rodney several months into the second season.

The writing staff gather at a series celebration on a soundstage in 1965. Pictured (left to right): Dick DeRoy, Sonya Roberts, Michael Gleason, Nina Laemmlie, Lionel Siegel, Paul Monash, Carol Sobieski, Celia Armanda (assistant to Paul Monash), and seated: Peggy Shaw, Rita Lakin, and Del Reisman.
Not pictured: John Wilder, Jerry Ziegman, and Ann Marcus.

Jeffrey Hayden became the series third director during the second season (1965–1966).

Ted Post, Dr. Ray Weston, Dorothy Malone, David Gerber and Esther Maloney (Dorothy Malone's mother) in late 1965 shortly after Malone's return to the series having recovered from a life-threatening illness.

Susan Oliver joined the cast as Ann Howard, who returns to *Peyton Place* to resolve a childhood incident that has haunted her for years. Her storyline took place during the last half of season two.

The women of *Peyton Place* in the spring of 1966. Top row: Barbara Parkins (Betty Anderson), Dorothy Malone (Constance MacKenzie Carson), Patricia Morrow (Rita Jacks Harrington), Evelyn Scott (Ada Jacks), Ruth Warrick (Hannah Cord). Bottom: Susan Oliver (Ann Howard) and Lana Wood (Sandy Webber).

The core cast of the series at the start of the third season (1966–1967). Seated on the bench from left: Barbara Parkins, Dorothy Malone, and Patricia Morrow. Top row standing from left: Ed Nelson, James Douglas, Ryan O'Neal, Tim O'Connor, and Christopher Connelly. The show debuted in color on September 12, 1966.

Ed Nelson (Dr. Michael Rossi) with director Lee Philips who portrayed high school principal Michael Rossi in the original feature film version of Peyton Place in 1957.

Chris Webber (Gary Haynes) hesitates turning back the clock seventeen years to find out who caused the accident that resulted in his blindness.

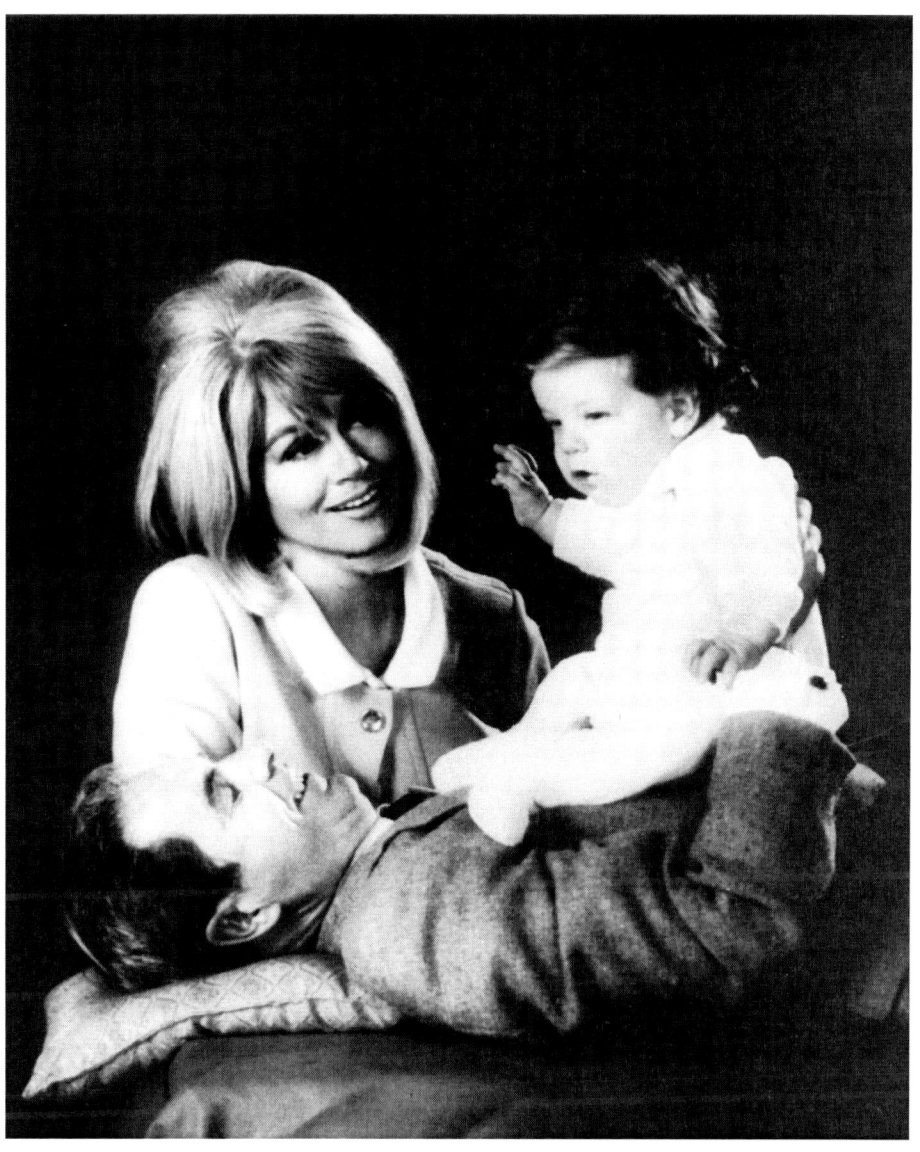

Elliot (Tim O'Connor) and Constance Carson (Dorothy Malone) with son Mathew (Michael Rubin) who arrived at the outset of season three in September of 1966. According to California law, Rubin (the son of actress Kathleen Hughes and producer Stanley Rubin) could only work two hours a day, and was not allowed to labor for more than 20 minutes. Because of the intensity of the lights, he could only be before the camera for 30 second takes. A social worker stood by with a stop watch.

Rachel Welles (Leigh Taylor-Young) who holds a possible link to the disappearance of Allison MacKenzie, is menaced by Jack Chandler (John Kellogg)—her uncle by marriage—during the series third year.

Ryan O'Neal (Rodney Harrington) and Leigh Taylor-Young (Rachel Welles) prepare to film a scene on the *Peyton Place* square in 1967.

Wilfred Hyde-White temporarily replaced George Macready as Martin Peyton during the latter's illness in 1967.

Con man Eddie Jacks (Dan Duryea) the estranged father/husband, irons his own shirt as *Peyton Place* begins its fourth season in September of 1967.

Steven Cord (James Douglas) is drawn to Adrienne Van Leyden (Gena Rowlands) who arrives in Peyton Place at Martin Peyton's request to breakup the marriage of Steven and Betty Cord.

Severely wounded Lee Webber (Stephen Oliver) is determined to exact revenge on employer Martin Peyton (George Macready) who betrayed him during season four in January of 1968.

Michael Christian debuted as Joe Rossi (Michael's younger brother) on the run from a incident in New York in February of 1968.

Constance (Dorothy Malone) and Elliot Carson (Tim O'Connor) make their exit in late May of 1968, when Elliot is offered a job opportunity in another town.

Barbara Rush, Ed Nelson and Elizabeth Walker at a social event in 1968. Rush (who portrayed Marsha Russell) and Walker (as daughter Carolyn) became principal players after the Carson's departure.

Carolyn Russell (Elizabeth Walker) and Joe Rossi (Michael Christian) take a joy ride at the Founder's Day Festival in Peyton Square in late spring of 1968.

Susan Winter (Diana Hyland) resents her husband Tom (Robert Hogan) being a minister and neglecting her needs as the show moved toward the end of season four.

High school senior Carolyn Russell (Elizabeth Walker) is conflicted over her parent's divorce and resentful of her mother's relationship with Dr. Rossi in the final season.

Neurosurgeon Harry Miles (Percy Rodriguez) first appears during the aftermath of Rodney Harrington's motorcycle accident in late July of 1968.

Alma Miles (Ruby Dee) is Harry's wife who makes her debut in early October of season five. Time was taken to develop the character of Harry Miles before introducing his family two months later.

Lew Miles (Glynn Turman) arrives in *Peyton Place* on October 14, 1968 as the troubled son who experienced a traumatic incident in New York that he keeps secret from his parents.

Rita Harrington (Patricia Morrow) and mother Ada Jacks (Evelyn Scott) beam smiles of delight as they watch a family reunion between Jill Smith (Joyce Jillson) and Joe Rossi (Michael Christian) with todler Kelly during season five in late October of 1968.

Rodney Harrington (Ryan O'Neal) ponders his fate during season five after being partially paralyzed in a motorcycle accident (at the end of season four in late summer of 1968). O'Neal would leave the show March 3rd, 1969, thirteen episodes before the series finale.

Rodney Harrington's (Ryan O'Neal) slow recovery concerns wife Betty (Barbara Parkins), as well as his brother Norman (Christopher Connelly) and his wife, Rita (Patricia Morrow).

Maggie Riggs (Florida Friebus) was introduced during season five. She became Eli Carson's companion and they were later engaged.

The original watercolor of the *Peyton Place* square by 20th Century Fox illustrator Stan Johnson. Pictured left to right: The Antique Store, MacKenzie Book Gallery, Peyton Place Real Estate Office, Jewelry Store, Peyton Professional Building, *The Clarion*, and Ships Chandlery.

The square was constructed at the north end of the 20th Century Fox main lot where a park existed. The series of shops in the illustration were built on the west side because they received natural light exposure for most of the day. The display windows in all of the shops were tilted to prevent light reflection. The town square was always shot at specific angles so as not to reveal the looming construction of Century City just north of the studio.

```
Picture Started September 30, 1963                 Construct: Department Report                    October 18, 1963

6006                                    "PEYTON PLACE"
Paul Monash  - Executive Producer       Irvin Kershner - Director              W. Simonds - Art Director
Gaston Glass - Unit Manager             J. Gertsman - Assistant Director       J. Richter - Key Grip
Carl Guthrie - Cameraman
```

SET NO.	DESCRIPTION	DATE SHOT	STAGE	OTHER
6006-01	INT. & EXT. DINER	10/1-9		WESTERN AVENUE
6006-02	INT. SWAIN'S OFFICE	ELIMINATED		
6006-03	INT. CATHERINE'S BEDROOM	ELIMINATED		
6006-04	INT. HARRINGTON'S STAIR HALL	9/30		WESTERN AVENUE
6006-05	INT. MACKENZIE'S HOME - U.F.	ELIMINATED		
6006-06	INT. DRESS SHOP	9/30 10/1		WESTERN AVENUE
6006-07	INT. & EXT. MACKENZIE'S HOME - L.F.	10/7-9		
6006-08	INT. & EXT. CROSS HOME	10/2	8	WESTERN AVENUE
6006-09	INT. HARRINGTON'S BREAKFAST ROOM	10/4-7-9		SOUND DEPARTMENT
6006-10	EXT. TOWN SQUARE	10/2		WESTERN AVENUE
6006-11	INT. SCHOOL ROOM	ELIMINATED		
6006-12	INT. HARRINGTON'S OFFICE	10/8	3	
6006-13	INT. ANDERSON'S HOME	10/10	11	OLD SPECIAL EFFECTS BLDG.
6006-14	INT. ROADHOUSE	ELIMINATED		CAFE
6006-15	EXT. RAILROAD STATION	10/8		NEAR PRODUCTION BUNGALOW
6006-16	EXT. SIGNS	10/3		STUDIO CITY
6006-17	EXT. HARRINGTON'S MILL	10/10		NEAR STABLE AREA
6006-18	EXT. MACKENZIE'S HOUSE	ELIMINATED (See 24)		
6006-19	EXT. RAILROAD TRACKS	10/10	15	
6006-20	EXT. ACCIDENT	10/9-10	15	
6006-21	EXT. MACKENZIE HOME	10/10		NEAR STABLES
6006-22	EXT. RODNEY'S CAR (PROCESS)	10/11		NEAR OLYMPIC BRIDGE
6006-23	EXT. ROAD			
6006-24	EXT. COUNTRY HIGHWAY ACCIDENT			

F I N A L   R E P O R T

The set construction report for the pilot and preview scenes filmed from September 30th to October 10th of 1963. Irvin Kershner directed from a script written by Paul Monash.

CONSTRUCTION   October 14, 1965

7737   "PEYTON PLACE"   Location

01   INT. HOSPITAL CORRIDOR & ROSSI'S OFFICE   9
02   INT. HOSPITAL CORRIDOR - U.F.   9
03   INT. BOSTON CLINIC   15
04   INT. BOYS' APARTMENT   4
05   INT. COURTROOM CORRIDOR   4

7739

01   INT. COURTHOUSE CORRIDOR   4
02   INT. FOWLER'S OFFICE
03   INT. ROSSI'S OFFICE   9

7741

01   EXT. SQUARE   Lot
02   INT. HOSPITAL - MORTON'S OFFICE   9
03   INT. COURTHOUSE - FOWLER'S OFFICE   3
04   INT. ADA JACKS' LIVING QUARTERS   12

7742

01   INT. DOCTOR'S HOSPITAL CORRIDOR   9
02   INT. HARRINGTON BOYS' APARTMENT   4
03   INT. INN - DINING AREA   12

7743

01   INT. HOSPITAL CORRIDOR, ALLISON'S ROOM & ROSSI'S OFFICE   9
02   EXT. WHARF   Lot
03   EXT. DOWELL'S GARDEN   Old Writers' Bldg.
04   INT. ADA JACKS' TAVERN

7746

01   INT. FOWLER HOUSE   12
02   INT. DOWELL'S WAITING ROOM   7
03   REPAIR CLOCK - PEYTON SQUARE   Square

7745

01   INT. HOSPITAL CORRIDOR   9
02   EXT. PLAYGROUND   Old Writers' Bldg.
03   INT. FOWLER'S OFFICE   12

7747

01   INT. DOCTOR'S HOSPITAL   9
02   INT. SCHUSTER'S HOUSE   3
03   INT. HARRINGTON BOYS' APARTMENT   4

                    F I N A L   R E P O R T

A set construction report from an early second season episode in October of 1965. Many of the permanent sets which included the hospital corridor and Rossi's office, MacKenzie home and Anderson home existed on stage 9.

SET CONSTRUCTION   February 17, 1966
"PEYTON PLACE"

No.	Description	Location
7899	(AMORTIZED)	
01	EXT. PEYTON PLACE SHORE LINE	Shore Line
02	INT. GENERAL STORE	4
03	INT. EMPTY ROOM	7
04	INT. ROSSI'S BEACH HOUSE	7
05	EXT. BLUFF	Shore Line
06	EXT. BLUFF - STAGE	4
07	EXT. GENERAL STORE (Trans. from 01)	Square
08	INT. GARAGE	9
09	EXT. GARAGE	Wharf
10	INT. CLARION	9
7800		
01	INT. MacKENZIE HOUSE	9
02	INT. NORM & RITA'S APARTMENT	4
03	INT. INN LOBBY	12
04	INT. CLARION OFFICE	9
05	INT. ANDERSON LIVING ROOM	9
06	INT. ROD'S CELL	9
07	INT. PEYTON LIVING ROOM	3
7801		
01	EXT. SQUARE	Square
02	INT. COURTHOUSE CORRIDOR	4
03	INT. PEYTON HOUSE	3
04	INT. MacKENZIE HOUSE	9
05	INT. INN - ROD'S ROOM	3
06	EXT. PEYTON HOUSE	Tenn. Gate
07	INT. MILL - SCHUSTER'S OFFICE	3
08	INT. DRESS SHOP	9
09	INT. ANDERSON HOUSE	9
10	INT. INN LOBBY	12
7803		
01	EXT. SQUARE	Square
02	INT. ANDERSON'S HOUSE - BETTY'S BEDROOM	9
03	INT. NORM & RITA'S APARTMENT	4
04	INT. PEYTON HOUSE	3
05	EXT./INT. MacKENZIE HOUSE	9
06	EXT. PEYTON HOUSE (ADDITION)	Tenn. Gate
07	EXT. WHARF	Shore Line
08	EXT. SAIL BOAT	Shore Line
09	(CANCELED)	--
10	(Transferred to 7899)	--
11	INT. MacKENZIE BEDROOM	9

F I N A L   R E P O R T

Set construction report from February of 1966 (second year mid-season). Many of the remaining interiors not filmed on stage 9 were shot on stages 3, 4, 7 and 12 as indicated here and in the subsequent report. The budget for a thirty minute episode was approximately $60,000.

SET CONSTRUCTION
"PEYTON PLACE"

April 1, 1966

No.	Description	Location
7811		
01	INT. DOWELL'S OUTER OFFICE & STEVEN'S OFFICE	7
02	INT. DRUG STORE	7
03	INT. CIDER BARREL	Shore Line
04	INT. PEYTON HOUSE	3
7812		
01	INT. HOSPITAL THERAPY ROOM	9
02	INT. PEYTON HOUSE	3
03	INT. INN - STEVEN'S ROOM	3
04	INT. TAVERN LIVING QUARTERS	12
05	EXT. GARAGE	Shore Line
06	INT. GENERAL STORE	4
07	INT. CLARION	9
7813		
01	EXT. PEYTON HOUSE	Tenn. Gate
02	INT. PEYTON HOUSE	3
03	INT. HOSPITAL	9
04	EXT. SQUARE	Peyton Sq.
05	INT. DRUG STORE	7
06	INT. RITA & NORM'S APARTMENT	4
07	EXT. WHARF	Shore Line
08	INT. ROSSI'S BEACH HOUSE	4
09	EXT. HOSPITAL PARKING LOT	Adm. Bldg.
10	INT. GARAGE	9
11	INT. MORTON'S OFFICE	
7815		
01	INT. HSOPITAL	9
02	EXT. SQUARE	Peyton Sq.
03	INT. DRUG STORE	7
04	INT./EXT. GARAGE	9
05	INT. STEVEN & BETTY'S ROOM AT INN	3
06	INT. INN	12
07	INT. PEYTON BEDROOM	3
7817		
01	EXT. WHARF	Shore Line
02	EXT. RODNEY'S GARAGE	Shore Line
03	INT. RODNEY'S GARAGE	9
04	INT. HOSPITAL	9
05	INT. PEYTON HOUSE	3
06	INT. PEYTON BEDROOM	3
07	INT. STEVEN & BETTY'S ROOM	7
08	EXT. PEYTON HOUSE	Tenn. Gate

Set construction report from April, 1966. Notice that the Tennessee gate of the studio was used as an exterior for the Peyton Mansion which was a facade. Several of the studio structures including the Administration Building, Old Writers Building, Commissary and Machine Shop were used as exteriors in the series as well as the parking lots. Very seldom did the series venture off of the studio lot in west Los Angeles.

Broadcast History

BROADCAST PERIODS

September 1964–June 1965	*Tuesday/Thursday, 9:30–10 PM*
June 1965–October 1965	*Tuesday/Thursday/Friday, 9:30-10 PM*
November 1965–August 1966	*Monday/Tuesday/Thursday, 9:30-10 PM*
September 1966–January 1967	*Monday/Wednesday, 9:30-10 PM*
January 1967–August 1967	*Monday/Tuesday, 9:30-10 PM*
September 1967–Sept. 1968	*Monday/Thursday, 9:30-10 PM*
September 1968–January 1969	*Monday/Wednesday, 8:30-9 PM*
February 1969–June 1969	*Monday, 8:30-9 PM*

PRINCIPLE CAST

Constance MacKenzie/Carson (1964–1968) Dorothy Malone
Matthew Swain (1964–1965) Warner Anderson
Dr. Michael Rossi (1964–1969) Ed Nelson
Allison MacKenzie (1964–1966) Mia Farrow
Rodney Harrington (1964–1969) Ryan O'Neal
Betty Anderson/Cord/Harrington (1964–1969) Barbara Parkins
Norman Harrington (1964–1969) Christopher Connelly
Leslie Harrington (1964–1968) Paul Langton
Julie Anderson (1964–1966) Kasey Rogers

George Anderson (1964–1965) Henry Beckman
Laura Brooks (1964–1965) Patricia Breslin
Catherine Harrington (1964) Mary Anderson
Dr. Robert Morton (1964–1966) Kent Smith
Paul Hanley (1965) Richard Evans
Eli Carson (1965–1969) Frank Ferguson
Elliot Carson (1965–1968) Tim O'Connor
Dr. Claire Morton (1965) Mariette Hartley
Steven Cord (1965–1969) James Douglas
Dr. Vincent Markham/Kenneth Markham (1965) Leslie Nielsen
Rita Jacks/Harrington (1965–1969) Patricia Morrow
Ada Jacks (1965–1969) Evelyn Scott
David Schuster (1965–1966) William Smithers
Doris Schuster (1965) Gail Kobe
Kim Schuster (1965) Kimberly Beck
Joe Chernak (1965) Don Quine
Stella Chernak (1965–1966) Lee Grant
Gus Chernak (1965–1966) Bruce Gordon
Russ Gehring (1965) David Canary
John Fowler (1965–1966) John Kerr
Marian Fowler (1965–1966) Joan Blackman
Martin Peyton (1965–1968) George Macready
Hannah Cord (1965–1967) Ruth Warrick
Constance MacKenzie (temporary replacement–1965) Lola Albright
Lee Webber (1966–1968) Stephen Oliver
Sandy Webber (1966–1967) Lana Wood
Chris Webber (1966–1967) Gary Haynes
Ann Howard (1966) Susan Oliver
Rachel Welles (1966–1967) Leigh Taylor-Young
Jack Chandler (1966–1967) John Kellogg
Adrienne Van Leyden (1967) Gena Rowlands
Eddie Jacks (1967–1968) Dan Duryea
Martin Peyton (temporary replacement 1967) Wilfred Hyde-White
Joe Rossi (1968) Michael Christian
Jill Smith (1968) Joyce Jillson
Rev. Tom Winter (1968–1969) Robert Hogan

Susan Winter (1968–1969) Diana Hyland
Marsha Russell (1968–1969) Barbara Rush
Carolyn Russell (1968–1969) Elizabeth Walker
Dr. Harry Miles (1968–1969) Percy Rodriguez
Fred Russell (1968–1969) Joe Maross
Alma Miles (1968–1969) Ruby Dee
Lew Miles (1968–1969) Glynn Turman
Joanne Walker (1968–1969) Jeanne Buckley
Maggie Riggs (1968–1969) Florida Friebus
Jeff Kramer (1968–1969) John Findlater
Vicki Fletcher (1969) Judy Pace

SECONDARY CAST

Dr. Joe Bradley (1964) Charles Irving
Sharon Purcell (1965) Danya Ceder
Roy Roberts (1965) Sherwood Price
Calvin Hanley (1965) Whit Bissell
Kitch Brunner (1965) Mickey Dolenz
Grace Morton (1965) Edith Atwater
Detective Blaine (1965) Myron Healey
Dr. Kessler (1965) John Zaremba
E. J. Taggart (1965) Dabbs Greer
Mr. Wainwright (1965) Gregory Morton
Detective Lawrence (1965–1966) Burt Remsen
Theodore Dowell (1965–1966) Patrick Whyte
Mrs. Chernak (1965) Anna Karen
Rev. Jerry Bedford (1965) Ted Hartley
Andrea Dowell (1965) Heather Angel
Nurse Choate (1965–1968) Erin O'Brien Moore
Sgt. Ed Goddard (1965–1968) Garry Walberg
Sgt. William Walker (1965–1969) Morris Buchanan
Judge Jessup (1965–1966) Curt Conway
Officer Frank (1965–1966) Greg Morris
Richard Jensen (1966) Don Gordon

Thomas (1965–1966) James Doohan
Ann Nolan (1965–1968) Penelope Gillette
Mrs. Hewitt (1965–1968) Maxine Stuart
Judge Chester (1966–1967) Jon Lormer
William Wainwright (1966–1968) Paul Newlan
Mary (1966–1968) Rose Hobart
William Kennerly (1967) Russell Thorson
Charlie (1967–1969) Frank London
Chuck Atwell (1968–1969) Mario Alcalde
William Kennerly, Jr. (1968) Don Dubbins
Donna Franklin (1968) Sharon Hugueny
Jennifer Ivers (1969) Myrna Fahey
Judge (1969) Michael Strong
Asst. D.A. Jerry Carter (1969) William Sargent

Peyton Place
Season One Summation
(September 15, 1964–September 10, 1965)

DR. MICHAEL ROSSI arrives in the small New England town of Peyton Place (population 9,875) after purchasing the practice of the late Donald Brooks (his classmate in medical school) from his widow Laura.

Laura Brooks is the sister of Leslie Harrington who manages the Peyton Mill. Leslie is unhappily married to Catherine Peyton, the daughter of influential patriarch Martin Peyton who owns the mill and lives two hours away in Boston. (His ancestor Samuel Peyton, is the founding father of Peyton Place.)

Michael is met at the train station by Leslie and Catherine's son Rodney Harrington, twenty, and his girlfriend Betty Anderson, seventeen, who drive him to the Colonial Post Inn in the center of town. Leslie Harrington is having an affair with his secretary Julia Anderson (Betty's mother).

When Rodney sees them embracing, it causes a sudden change in his feelings toward Betty.

Rodney then encounters high school senior Allison MacKenzie, seventeen, the shy and innocent friend of his younger brother Norman, seventeen, who lives in the shadow of his handsome and athletic older brother. Rodney is drawn to Allison whose over-protective mother Constance MacKenzie owns the town bookstore. Constance (Connie) supposedly a widow who has never remarried, has kept secret the true identity of Allison's father. Her closest male confident is distant cousin Matthew Swain (Matt), the editor of the Peyton Place Clarion. Allison too shares a closeness with Matt and contributes articles to the newspaper. Matt continually urges a reluctant Connie to reveal the truth to Allison about her father.

Meanwhile, turmoil exists in the Anderson household. George Anderson (Betty's father), a salesman for the Peyton Mill, is an alcoholic and physically abusive husband. Yet George loves his daughter and wants the best for her.

When George asks Michael Rossi for medication to curb his anger, Michael recommends that George see a psychiatrist in Boston. George is unreceptive and eventually receives tranquilizers.

Leslie Harrington, an ambitious and somewhat ruthless man with a weakness for his two sons, desires to leave his wife Catherine for Julie Anderson, but Julie refuses and quits her job at the mill. Although she no longer loves George, she feels a sense of guilt and reluctance to leave him. George plans to quit his sales position with the mill and intends to buy an insurance agency in town with Julie as his secretary.

Rodney begins dating Allison and rebuffs Betty who tries to find out why his feelings have changed.

During a routine physical, Michael Rossi discovers that Betty is pregnant. Betty is reluctant to tell Rodney for fear he might feel she's trying to trap him into a relationship. However, as her jealousy of Allison and longing for Rodney intensify, Betty confronts Rodney with her pregnancy at the Peyton Place Founders Festival. Rodney is shocked and on their drive back to town, they're involved in an automobile accident. As a result, Betty loses the baby but doesn't tell Rodney who feels guilty and proposes marriage. George Anderson sees opportunities for the Andersons once his daughter becomes a Harrington, and encourages Betty to maintain her secret. Rodney and Betty elope and are married a month after the accident.

Betty is not well received by her in-laws. Both Leslie and

Catherine Harrington disapprove of Betty and Catherine is disdainful. Norman is the only family member who tries to be supportive.

Rodney meets Allison and proclaims his feelings for her even though he is married and believes he will become a father.

At one point, an unhappy Betty attempts to leave Peyton Place but Allison persuades her to stay.

Laura Brooks stays on as Michael Rossi's secretary and develops an attraction for the New York doctor. However, Michael is interested romantically in Connie and they begin dating.

Michael has been renting the Carson cottage where eighteen years before, Elizabeth Carson was murdered, supposedly by her husband Elliot Carson. Elliot is currently in prison. On a visit to the cottage (during an evening with Michael) Connie becomes uncomfortable and reluctant to discuss the Carsons, mentioning she was in New York at the time of the murder.

Eli Carson, the proprietor of the Ships Chandlery, informs Michael that son Elliot is up for parole, may be released soon, and will return to Peyton Place to prove his innocence. If so, Eli wants his son to live in his old house again.

Later, during an evening with Michael, Connie reveals that the photograph of Allison's father in her living room is that of a stranger. However, she doesn't divulge the identity of Allison's true father.

Michael is then summoned to the Harrington mansion where Catherine has taken seriously ill. Catherine's personal physician, Dr. Robert Morton (chief-of-staff at Doctor's Hospital) is out of town. Rossi examines Catherine, believes she may have a perforated ulcer, and wants to admit her to the hospital for further testing.

Morton is notified in Boston, leaves immediately, and instructs Rossi to wait until he returns to Peyton Place.

Catherine's condition worsens at the hospital. Michael seeks help from other doctors but none are available. Rossi tells

Leslie Harrington that he must operate to save Catherine's life. Leslie finally gives consent and Rossi proceeds. Morton returns, scrubs up and enters the operating room, attempting to take control. Michael refuses and continues to operate. Catherine dies on the table. Morton faults Michael and intends to drive him out of Peyton Place.

Michael insists upon an autopsy to determine the cause of death, but is unable to get a postponement when he is called upon to treat Eli Carson for a sudden angina attack.

After Catherine's death, Betty informs Rodney that she lost the baby as a result of the car accident. Leslie confronts her about giving Rodney a divorce and wants her out of the house; but Betty has hired a lawyer. Leslie urges George and Julie Anderson to persuade Betty, but George is not supportive.

A medical inquisition of Michael Rossi is called by Robert Morton who claims Michael operated on Catherine Harrington without proper medical consultation. The medical review board determines that the operation was unnecessary. Michael's hospital privileges are suspended and his private practice patients begin to cancel their appointments.

Michael is determined to prove his innocence. At the hospital he demands to see the tissue samples of Catherine's pancreas and the ulcer, but Dr. Joe Bradley (the pathologist who testified against him at the medical inquisition) is evasive.

Michael discovers through Laura Brooks that Bradley was once a surgeon. He last operated five years before on Matt Swain. Donald Brooks (her husband) and Robert Morton assisted him.

Bradley feels pressured from Michael's investigation and confesses to Morton that he lied at the autopsy hearing. Rossi's diagnosis was correct. Catherine had a perforated ulcer. Bradley felt obligated to support Morton who helped save his career after his last operation. Morton is shocked by what his pathologist has done. Bradley resigns and Michael is reinstated at the hospital. Morton apologizes and offers to help Michael undo any damage done to his reputation.

Catherine's will is read and a codicil (an amendment) provides that all of her stock in the Peyton Mill will revert to her father, Martin Peyton. Leslie intends to fight the codicil. He asks Robert Morton to state that Catherine was disturbed when she wrote the amendment, but Morton refuses.

George Anderson's insurance business doesn't do well. During a drunken rage he attacks Julie who strikes him with a telephone. George is treated by Michael at the hospital and then released. Julie moves out of the house and goes to stay with Connie and Allison.

Betty has left Peyton Place for Boston and eventually goes to New York, hoping to get a fresh start. She meets Sharon Purcell (a woman of questionable character) who befriends her and takes Betty in as a temporary roommate.

Sharon arranges a date for Betty with Roy Roberts, a well-to-do businessman who misinterprets Betty's motives and makes a strong sexual overture. Betty becomes very upset and Roberts realizes he has misinterpreted her. He gives Betty money to return home and leaves.

Elliot Carson is paroled from prison with help from Matthew Swain, and returns to Peyton Place. Connie is uneasy about Elliot's return and confesses to Michael that Elliot is Allison's father. Connie feels if Elliot did kill Elizabeth, she might have been the cause of it.

Elliot moves back into his cottage and Michael moves to the Colonial Post Inn.

Elliot and Allison meet and find common interests in writing, reading and literature.

George Anderson's condition begins to worsen. His insurance business fails, and he owes rent. He continues drinking, accusing his wife of infidelity, and starts hallucinating. He barricades himself in his office with a loaded gun and shoots the phone when it rings. Elliot is able to get inside by engaging George in conversation about their respective military service experiences. Elliot manages to disarm George and (with Michael Rossi) escorts him to the Greenvale Sanitarium for treatment for manic depression.

Laura Brooks decides to leave Peyton Place and travel in Europe. Michael offers her job to Julie Anderson who refuses Leslie's offer to return to the mill and resume her old position.

While buying medication for his father Eli, Elliot encounters pharmacy owner Calvin Hanley, his former father-in-law. Elliot proclaims his innocence in Elizabeth's death, but Calvin insists he is guilty.

Elliot also encounters his ex-brother-in-law, Paul Hanley, who testified against Elliot at his trial, and was instrumental in sending him to prison. Paul teaches freshman English at Peyton College and is also a faculty advisor to Allison. Elliot feels Paul is a twisted, resentful man. Both he and Connie disapprove of Paul's association with Allison. When Paul desires to take Allison on a field trip, Connie refuses to let her go.

Elliot is determined to prove his innocence. He confronts Calvin Hanley with the fact that Elizabeth was involved with Leslie Harrington, and that someone planted the idea in Paul that Elliot killed his sister. A tension exists between Paul and his father Calvin. Paul is unsure about his testimony that helped convict Elliot and feels that his father forced him to lie about Elliot.

After his confrontation with Elliot, Calvin confronts Leslie Harrington about his affair with Elizabeth. Leslie denies it but Calvin threatens to destroy his reputation. However, a short time later Calvin dies of a heart attack.

Betty Anderson returns to Peyton Place, disillusioned by her experiences in New York. She makes a deal with Leslie and agrees to an annulment of her marriage to Rodney in exchange for hospital care for her father. Leslie gives a detective's report on Betty's activities in New York to Rodney to insure he has no second thoughts about a reconciliation. Rodney doesn't like the idea that his father spied on Betty rather than trying to find her. He tears up the report, but it causes friction between him and his soon-to-be ex-wife.

Betty is unsure of what to do with her life. During a visit to

Michael Rossi's office, she displays a nice rapport with an upset injured child. Michael suggests that Betty pursue a job at the hospital as a nurse's aide. Head Nurse Choate is not impressed with Betty, feels she is troubled and irresponsible, and is against hiring her. Choate is rude and hostile toward Betty. She gives her a difficult time during the course of her training; but Robert Morton ratifies Betty's appointment.

Once the annulment is finalized, Rodney and Allison resume dating.

One night at the Shoreline Café (a teen hangout near the wharf), Norman Harrington meets Rita Jacks whom he knows from high school. Rita is a working class girl and the daughter of Ada Jacks who runs a tavern on the wharf. Rita is with boyfriend Kitch Brunner and some of his friends. Kitch dislikes the Harringtons and has it in for Norman. He gets Rita to invite Norman over to their table and spikes his drink. Once Rita knows what Kitch has done, she tries to get Norman to leave without success. When Norman does leave the café stumbling along, Kitch and his friends follow. They jump Norman, rough him up and tie him to the pillory in the square.

Rodney finds out what Kitch Brunner has done and decides to avenge his brother. He finds Kitch and his friend Earl working on the wharf. They goad Rodney into a fight thinking they have the advantage. Earl swings at Rodney, just missing his head. Rodney hits Earl, knocking him down, and hits him again as he starts to get up. Kitch throws Rodney to the ground and hits him several times. Rodney retaliates with a combination which floors Kitch who doesn't get up. Rodney warns the two wharf rats to stay away from Norman, and walks away as they both lie there.

Leslie proceeds with plans to contest Catherine's will and prove that his wife was incompetent. Norman resents what his father plans to do and vows to fight him in court.

Elliot continues in his quest to find out who killed his wife Elizabeth. Paul Hanley discovers his sister's diary and secretly leaves it at the cottage for Elliot to discover. In reading it, Elliot learns that Elizabeth was seeing Leslie and that Catherine Harrington probably knew about it. On the night of her death, Leslie was coming to the cottage to discuss the matter. However, Elizabeth felt Leslie was a "good catch" and had no intention of breaking off their relationship. Elliot believes Leslie killed Elizabeth during a confrontation.

Once Leslie becomes aware of the diary, he pressures Connie to persuade Elliot to hand it over to him. If not, he threatens to reveal Elliot as Allison's real father. Connie refuses to help Leslie and cautions Elliot to hold onto the diary which could help prove his innocence.

Elliot is later served a subpoena ordering him to appear in court at the contesting of Catherine Harrington's will and produce the diary. Elliot considers destroying it to protect Allison but he's persuaded by Matt Swain to meet with Leslie and prevent the hearing.

Elliot offers Leslie a deal. He won't allow attorney William Wainwright to use the diary against Leslie if he agrees not to bother Connie again. Leslie agrees and on the advice of his attorney Theodore Dowell, drops his opposition to the codicil, as the diary could still turn into a murder investigation. Wainwright (Martin Peyton's lawyer who had been helping Elliot) then offers Leslie a settlement in return for a letter of resignation.

Paul Hanley is continually haunted by his part in sending Elliot to prison and becomes obsessed with Leslie's guilt. Soon after Leslie drops his case, Paul finds a way to exact his revenge via George Anderson.

George has returned to Peyton Place for a trial visit, unhappy with Betty's annulment and the deal she made with Leslie Harrington. George meets Leslie at his office, promises to pay back the medical costs and blames Leslie for being confined at the sanitarium. He leaves, highly frustrated and resentful, and meets Paul who is well aware of the enmity between the two men. Paul offers to buy George a drink at Ada Jack's tavern. George is reluctant but Paul persists.

While George gets drunk, Paul makes Ada confirm that Leslie had an affair with Elizabeth, and suggests Leslie had several affairs including one with Julie Anderson. George becomes agitated and decides to punish Leslie. Meanwhile Julie notifies Elliot (who brought George back from the sanitarium) that George is missing. Elliot learns from Ada Jacks that George has gone to Leslie's mansion. Elliot calls Leslie to warn him.

Paul has driven George to the Harrington home. George breaks in but Leslie is on the alert and defends himself with a hand gun. George is able to trick Leslie, gain possession of his weapon, and demand Leslie write a confession stating he murdered Elizabeth.

Elliot manages to enter the house and sees what is happening. He attempts to interfere and George shots him. George becomes delusional and Leslie is able to grab his gun back. George is taken into police custody.

At the hospital, Michael Rossi discovers the bullet is lodged near Elliot's heart. Both he and Robert Morton operate to save Elliot.

Leslie visits Elliot in the hospital and promises to help clear his name. Then Elliot begins to hemorrhage and his condition worsens.

Constance reveals to Allison that Elliot is her biological father. Allison is shocked and runs out.

Elliot undergoes a second operation and survives. For a time Allison is resentful and avoids her mother. Elliot is able to mediate and Allison returns home.

Leslie meets with attorney Ted Dowell and confesses he saw Catherine that night at the cottage with a poker in her hand at about the time Elizabeth was killed. Leslie instructs Dowell to contact the Lt. Governor regarding his confession and a pardon for Elliot.

A subsequent newspaper article clears Leslie and Elliot. Leslie resigns from his position at the Peyton Mill. He subsequently leaves town to travel through Europe and meet his sister Laura Brooks.

Connie and Elliot decide to marry and go on a honeymoon.

Rodney and Norman move out of the mansion and into the Hanley apartment above the pharmacy.

Attorney Steven Cord (the son of Martin Peyton's housekeeper, Hannah Cord) returns to Peyton Place after a long absence. He brings with him a letter for attorney Theodore Dowell (from Martin Peyton) suggesting that Dowell take Steven into his practice as an associate. Stevens seems to harbor a resentment toward the Harringtons, and vows that one day the Harrington mansion will be his.

While working with Dowell, Steven meets Julie and Betty in the law office. Steven is attracted to Betty, eventually asks her out and they begin dating.

Dr. Claire Morton (Robert Morton's daughter) arrives in Peyton Place from Lima, Peru where she lived with her husband Dr. Vincent Markham. Vincent heads a humanitarian project there. Claire plans to divorce Vincent and joins the staff at Doctor's Hospital.

An attraction develops between Claire and Michael Rossi, but Vincent Markham finds out about Claire's plans to divorce him and he comes to Peyton Place. Enroute, Vincent is injured in a bus accident, and he's taken to Doctor's Hospital.

Michael operates on Vincent and, during his convalescence, discovers that Markham has a rare blood disease and could die if he returns to Peru.

Kenneth Markham (Vincent's twin brother), an industrialist from Philadelphia, arrives in town to see his brother. Claire decides not to go through with divorce proceedings because of Vincent's illness. Kenneth offers Vincent a position with his foundation to keep his brother from leaving the country, but Vincent refuses. Ultimately Vincent receives a grant for his work in South America and plans to return there. Claire decides to go with him.

David Schuster, the new manager of the Peyton Mill, arrives in town with his wife Doris and pre-teenage daughter Kim who is deaf and very seldom speaks. The Schusters move into the mansion.

When Kim's teacher is unable to come to Peyton Place, Doris Schuster recommends that Kim be sent to a school for the deaf in Boston. Kim reads her lips and decides to run away. David believes Kim has fled because of their recent move and blames his wife who was in favor of it.

Allison finds Kim at the shore and, with Rodney, returns her to the mansion. Kim responds more favorably to Allison than to Doris and eventually David hires Allison as a permanent babysitter.

Elliot disapproves of the way David relates to Allison (who reminds him of his first wife), and takes an immediate dislike to him. Elliot's feelings intensify when David plans to automate the mill (which is losing money) and fire many of the town workers. Elliot writes an article in the Clarion criticizing David and holding him accountable. Elliot proposes a town meeting where the workers can voice their grievances and give David an opportunity to defend his position and address his future plans. Matt Swain has some issues with Elliot's critique but appreciates his sense of truth and concern for what is going on in Peyton Place.

Matt decides to leave town and suggests that Elliot replace him as the editor of the Clarion.

Doris Schuster grows resentful of Allison's bond with Kim, feeling it deprives her of spending much needed time with her daughter. Doris fires Allison despite David's objections. (After a replacement is fired, Allison is later asked to babysit when the Schusters host a dinner party to calm the tensions caused by David's planned changes at the mill.)

Norman Harrington has developed an interest in Rita Jacks who felt badly about the incident at the Shoreline Café. Rita is reluctant to date Norman. She feels beneath the Harringtons and Rodney is cool to her; but Norman convinces her of his genuine interest. However, conflict lies ahead for the couple.

Rita's old boyfriend Joe Chernak, a troublemaker (who recently did time on an honor farm for stealing a car) returns to town. Joe begins to stalk and harass Rita when she rejects his overtures.

Norman is determined to stand up for Rita. When he finds Joe is bothering Rita, he threatens him. Joe disregards Norman's warnings and is relentless. Several times he attempts to force himself upon Rita including the night of Norman's prom. Rita is left shaken, upset and confused as to what she should do. She fears for her safety as well as Norman's, but is reluctant to contact the police. At the same time, Rita's episodes with Joe arouse a suspicion and distrust in Norman that threatens their relationship.

Stella Chernak, Joe's older sister, returns to Peyton Place after a seven-year absence. (She recently worked as a biochemist at a medical facility in California.) Joe resents Stella's success and having to measure up to her. Still he seeks refuge in their relationship and asks Stella to leave town with him. Stella is aware of Joe's problems and doesn't see that as a solution.

When Norman gets a job at the wharf that Joe wanted, Joe taunts him about getting up close and personal with Rita the night of his prom. Joe is able to goad Norman into a fight and gives the smaller Harrington a beating.

Rodney finds out about the fight and goes looking for Joe, determined to bring an end to the torment he's caused his brother and Rita. He finds Joe on the wharf. Rodney tells Joe they're going to find Norman and that Joe is going to admit he lied about what took place between him and Rita the night of Norman's prom. Joe slugs Rodney but Rodney retaliates with a combination that sends Joe reeling. Joe realizes he might not win fighting fairly. He swings a heavy pulley (or block-and-tackle) slightly grazing Rodney. Rodney grabs it on the return swing. Joe grabs a crate and throws it at Rodney. Rodney picks up a gaffing hook and tells Joe he ought to jam it down his throat; but he doesn't have to fight Joe's way and deliberately tosses it over Joe's head. Joe, thinking otherwise, backs up, trips and falls into a boat hitting his head. Rodney offers to help but Joe spits at him. Joe gets up, climbs back on the wharf, and approaches Rodney. After a few steps he collapses. Rodney hurries over to a nearby pay phone and calls the hospital for an ambulance. Rodney goes back, kneels down and examines an unresponsive Joe. Rodney stands up and walks away. Two fishermen walk by and notice Joe's body. They realize he's dead and call the police.

Kim Shuster (who ran away from Allison and Norman at the library) has been hiding on the wharf and witnessed the fight. She flees. A short time later, Allison and Norman find her shaking and crying.

Joe Chernak is declared dead at the scene. Stella is trouble by her brother's death. She admits that Joe was a rotten troublemaker but feels guilty in her inability and unwillingness to help him. Joe wanted to go away with her to California and now she blames herself for his death.

Sgt. Ed Goddard questions Rita Jacks about Joe's demise.

Michael Rossi (who has been treating Stella's father Gus for cirrhosis) accompanies Stella to the Schuster house where her mother works as a servant. They inform Mrs. Chernak about Joe and she collapses.

—END OF SEASON ONE—

Peyton Place
Season Two Summation
(SEPTEMBER 14, 1965–SEPTEMBER 8, 1966)

STELLA CHERNAK informs the police that Rodney Harrington came looking for her brother Joe hours before his death.

At the police station, Rodney gives a voluntary confession (despite family lawyer Theodore Dowell's objections). He admits not calling police immediately after he realized Joe was dead because he panicked.

Allison MacKenzie believes that Kim witnessed Joe's death and tells the Schusters. David confronts his daughter but gets no response. However, when Allison questions her, Kim admits that Rodney made Joe fall to his death. David relates this to the police.

The Chernak's hostility toward Rodney intensifies. Gus blames the young Harrington for his son's death and assures Stella that he'll pay for it.

Stella tells Sgt. Goddard and D.A. John Fowler that Rodney hated Joe, threatened to kill him, and gives an official statement. Soon after, Rodney is arrested.

Leslie Harrington returns from Europe and Theodore Dowell advises him to remain in the background during the court proceedings. At that same time, Dowell admits he is not a criminal attorney and advises Leslie to find a high profile criminal attorney. Leslie is reluctant.

Meanwhile, Steven Cord has taken an interest in the case and feels John Fowler has an axe to grind regarding the Harringtons. (Leslie withheld evidence and Elliot Carson went to jail because of it.) Dowell is impressed with Steven's research of Fowler and allows Steven to work with him on Rodney's defense. (Ultimately, Steven becomes the lead attorney and Dowell resigns as Rodney's defense lawyer at Martin Peyton's request.)

Leslie makes peace with Norman but doesn't fare well with Elliot who refuses to forgive him.

At Rodney's hearing, Kim Schuster testifies that during their fight, Rodney made Joe Chernak fall by throwing a hook at him. Steven Cord counters that Rodney was actually throwing the hook away and not at Joe. Kim admits she doesn't know what was said.

Stella Chernak testifies under oath that Rodney threatened to kill Joe.

As a result, Rodney's case goes to trial.

Kim Schuster is left deeply troubled by her experience in court. Doris Schuster decides to return to New York where Kim can get proper help at the Institute. David Schuster remains alone in Peyton Place and visits them on the weekends.

Amidst all this, Allison is the victim of a hit-and-run accident and is hospitalized in a coma.

Leslie seeks help from Martin Peyton to finance Rodney's bail set at six figures. Peyton loathes Leslie for the way he treated daughter Catherine, but agrees to help his grandson.

Michael Rossi secures a hospital grant for his research project and offers Stella Chernak a job as a research assistant if she decides to remain in Peyton Place. Stella accepts the position.

Elliot Carson visits Allison in the hospital and reads to his daughter, hoping it will awaken her.

Rodney, out on bail, confronts Stella about her lying in court, but she refuses to acknowledge him. (Steven later admonishes Rodney for approaching a witness who has testified against him.)

Martin Peyton instructs Steven Cord to find evidence on Stella that he can use to discredit her. Steven contacts a detective named Lawrence whom he worked with at his prior law office.

While the police investigate Allison's hit-and-run accident, it's revealed that Marian Fowler is the driver who hit Allison. Marian works at the hospital as a volunteer in children's therapy. The night of the accident, Marian was coming from the home of physical therapist Russ Gehring. Marian deliberately rams her car into a garage post to cover up the damage done. When John Fowler finds out about her deception and infidelity, he demands a divorce and throws Marian out.

In an effort to help Rodney's case Betty removes a file on Stella Chernak from Nurse Choate's office and gives it to Steven, hoping to find evidence that might discredit her testimony. Once Steven makes copies, Betty is caught by Esther Choate replacing the file. Choate informs Michael Rossi who recommends that Betty resign (so that nothing will go on her record).

Martin Peyton, the seventy five-year-old patriarch of Peyton Place, returns for Rodney's trial, accompanied by his personal assistant, Hannah Cord. Peyton moves back into the mansion while David Schuster graciously moves to the Inn. Peyton opposes David's plan to automate the mill because it renders many of the workers unemployed. Their difference in the method of operation signals David's departure.

After three weeks in a coma, Allison awakens, free of brain damage, but with some paralysis and memory loss. She doesn't recognize Elliot as her father, or remember anything about her relationship with Rodney. Michael recommends that Dr. Quest, a psychiatrist, treat Allison (which angers her) and that Russ Gehring begin a physical therapy program.

Betty is introduced to Martin Peyton who is intrigued by her presence. Peyton sees drive and ambition in Betty and is not influenced by her past. He appreciates what she did for Rodney and offers her a job helping to care for him.

Michael Rossi and Stella Chernak socialize outside of the hospital but it doesn't get romantic because Stella is the chief witness against Rodney.

As the trial begins, Rita Jacks who hasn't wanted to get involved in Rodney's case, is called to testify. Steven is relentless in his questioning about Rita's personal relationship with Joe Chernak. Norman is infuriated by Steven's tactics and presiding Judge Jessup issues Steven a warning. Gus Chernak becomes enraged when Rita tells of Joe's violent behavior and he's ejected from the proceedings.

Gus pursues Rita to Ada's Tavern, refuses to leave, and an argument ensues. Stella enters and stops her father which triggers a confrontation between them later at home. Once there, Stella admits that Joe was a selfish rat and that both she and her father are frauds. Gus slaps her and forbids Stella to change one word of her testimony.

Shortly after Rita's episode in court, Norman proposes. They elope across state lines and get married in a nearby town. Rodney gives Rita and Norman the apartment above the pharmacy and moves out.

Back in court, Norman testifies, and Fowler tries to manipulate him into saying he asked Rodney to silence Joe, but Steven shows Norman's pride would never allow him to ask his brother for help.

Gus Chernak continues to act out his deep-seated resentment for the Harringtons and Martin Peyton. (During Leslie's tenure, Gus was removed from his job as loom operator and given the lesser position of night watchman. Most recently, David Schuster opted to give Rodney a job instead of Joe Chernak.)

After drinking, Gus attempts to destroy mill equipment by taking a sledgehammer to some of the machinery. David discovers Gus, restrains him and during a struggle Gus collapses.

At the hospital, Michael informs Gus that he has advanced cirrhosis and further drinking could be fatal. Gus (having been fired) leaves the hospital unannounced and seeks revenge against Martin Peyton. After drinking heavily, Gus breaks into the mansion and attempts to strike Martin Peyton with his cane, but collapses. Before he dies, Gus demands that Stella promise him Rodney will pay for Joe's death.

Allison continues to improve and is able to walk a bit. Rodney visits and they talk of their relationship and love for each other, but Allison's conflicts continue. She doesn't like being around Elliot and refuses to believe that he is her father. When Constance and Elliot visit her, Allison is rude and disrespectful. She confronts her mother with lying about her real father and sends them away.

Russ Gehring recognizes that Allison is spoiled, bored and lonely, so he pushes her in their therapy sessions to improve. At one point, Allison refuses to get out of her wheelchair. Russ is forceful and Allison reacts by subsequently cutting her hair.

Steven Cord learns from Detective Lawrence that Stella has a "checkered" past. While working as a biochemist at Westover Research Center in California, Stella was involved with a shipping clerk named Richard Jensen. Jensen was arrested one month before she quit her job as a result of a phone tip from an unidentified woman.

Marian Fowler returns to town after a disappearance, and confesses to her husband as to what occurred the day of Allison's hit-and-run accident. She had broken off her relationship with Russ Gehring and was driving back to town along the beach road. The sun was in her eyes and that is when she hit Allison. She thought she hit a rock or a small animal. John Fowler urges Marian to contact the police and accompanies her to the station.

At the station John encounters Russ Gehring (who had taunted him earlier regarding his affair with Marian). John realizes that Russ knew about Marian's accident and he "decks" Russ.

Russ is subsequently forced to resign from his job at the hospital and returns to Boston.

Allison's relationship with Constance and Elliot improves and she returns home to help her parents with preparation for the baby. (Constance has become pregnant.)

The trial ends and Rodney is found guilty of Joe Chernak's murder in the second degree. Allison, Betty, Norman, Elliot and Constance are all upset, while Martin Peyton vows to ruin Stella

Chernak. Steven is frustrated over losing the case and plans to appeal. At the same time, Steven arranges for Richard Jensen (the man from Stella's past) to come to Peyton Place. He hopes a confrontation with her past betrayal will force Stella to admit her current one—perjury.

Jensen arrives and holds Stella responsible for his incarceration. He attempts to blackmail her into stealing drugs from the hospital by threatening to reveal her history in California. Stella resists but is forced to steal from Michael Rossi's drug closet. However, she feels a strong sense of guilt and confesses to Michael. Jensen is arrested. Stella admits she lied about Rodney and contacts John Fowler to make a formal confession of perjury.

Michael bails Stella out of jail and soon after a hearing takes place. Stella later leaves town.

Once Rodney is freed, Betty admits to her mother Julie (who's been working at the mill as David Schuster's secretary) that she doesn't love Steven Cord because she still loves Rodney. Yet when Steven proposes, Betty decides to marry him.

Martin Peyton continues to manipulate the lives of the people around him. He offers Leslie the mill in exchange for having Rodney come to live with him in the mansion. Peyton wants an heir, Leslie is broke from the trial and accepts the offer. Rodney feels betrayed but agrees to live with his grandfather if he can remain in Peyton Place, get a job, and not go away to college.

Rodney buys the Shoreline Garage (with inheritance money) and hires a skilled mechanic named Lee Webber who worked for the previous owner. Lee is opinionated, abrasive, blunt and volatile. He advises Rodney on how to increase his profits by cutting corners, but Rodney disapproves of his tactics. An ongoing tension exists between the two. Lee is envious and resentful of Rodney's wealth and privilege. Had Lee not put his younger brother through college, he would have owned the garage.

Allison and Rodney resume dating and feelings get intense.

Allison talks of marriage but Rodney wants to be more secure and established to provide for her.

Betty and Steven get married at the mansion. Hannah Cord buys Steven a house, and Martin makes Steven his personal lawyer. Steven will handle all the legal business of the Peyton Mill, replacing Theodore Dowell who leaves town.

Over Steven's objections, Betty continues to work for Martin Peyton in the mansion where Rodney lives.

Norman goes to work for Eli Carson who opens a general store.

Enter Ann Howard who replaces Russ Gehring as the new physical therapist at the hospital. Ann has an unresolved and troubled past. She's continually haunted by memories of a tragic childhood incident while growing up in Peyton Place. Seventeen years before, Ann was accused of pushing Chris Webber (Lee's younger brother) from Sailor's Bluff to the shoreline rocks below, resulting in his blindness. Ann has never believed it was true and has come back to find out who was really responsible.

On a date with Michael Rossi, Ann explains what supposedly took place the day of Chris' accident. She was blindfolded by the other kids on the bluff, chased and pushed. In pushing back, she heard a scream, removed the blindfold and heard the other kids hollering that she had pushed Chris onto the rocks below where he lay bleeding. Steven Cord who blamed Ann like the other kids did, feels a sense of guilt and agrees to help her find the truth.

Both Hannah Cord and Martin Peyton are disturbed by Ann's return. Hannah secretly writes an anonymous "poison pen" letter to the Clarion about Ann, deeming her a threat to the handicapped children she works with because of the accident she purportedly caused seventeen years before. Hannah reveals to Martin her motivation in wanting to drive Ann out of Peyton Place. She's afraid that Steven will discover that Ann is his twin sister.

Lee Webber is also uncomfortable about Ann's return. He doesn't want Ann digging up the past and upsetting his brother.

Rodney meanwhile finds himself increasingly at odds with Lee Webber. At the Shoreline Café with Allison, Norman and Rita, Rodney is manipulated into dancing with an attractive and flirtatious woman named Sandy. It turns out Sandy is Lee's wife, and when Lee sees them dancing together, he slaps her. On another occasion when Sandy begs Lee to visit Chris, he becomes angry, attempts to strike her and is stopped by Rodney.

Sandy later admits to Rodney that she married Lee out of fear and feels he has bad intentions toward Ann Howard.

Chris Webber arrive in Peyton Place and Lee tries to isolate him from Ann. When Steven attempts to question Chris, Lee hits him.

Rodney and Allison begin to separate. Allison still wants to get married but Rodney feels it wouldn't last, that Allison exists half in reality, half in fantasy, and he needs reality.

Sandy Webber continually flirts with Rodney despite her jealous husband, and Rodney does his best to resist her because of Lee. Yet, she is relentless.

Ann Howard spends a lot of time with Michael Rossi and falls in love with him. Michael encourages her to stop living in the past.

Leslie Harrington wants to marry Julie Anderson but Julie decides to leave Peyton Place and go back to George who is making progress. Julie feels George needs her but Leslie doesn't.

Although Betty tries to make her marriage work, Steven Cord still believes that Betty is in love with Rodney and his jealousy is a strain on their relationship. Also troubling Steven is the true identity of his father and why both Hannah and Martin are hiding it from him.

Betty learns that Brian Colby (real name Brian Cord) was Steven's father, but is cautioned by Hannah not to reveal it.

Hannah destroys Catherine Peyton Harrington's painting with a knife and tries to place the blame on Ann, suggesting she broke into the mansion.

Steven confronts Hannah about her hostility toward Ann and demands answers about the paintings of Catherine found in

Brian Colby's trunk. (It's revealed that Catherine was an artist model for Colby and they had an affair.)

Ann learns that her father (Brian Colby) is in critical condition but he dies before she can see him. Steven is puzzled by the strange and frightened way his mother reacted to Brian Colby's imminent death, but gets no explanation.

Now that Betty knows her secret, Hannah wants her out of the mansion and tries to draw a wedge between her and Steven using Rodney. This causes more conflicts between Steven and Betty who walks out on him.

Chris Webber meets Allison at the Clarion. He's intrigued by her little girl voice and by the way she deals with his handicap. They find things in common. Allison becomes a reader to Chris, and the two spend time together.

Lee Webber confronts Ann Howard in a threatening manner and warns her to stop questioning Chris about the accident. Lee then instructs Chris on avoiding Ann. However, Ann is determined to speak further with Chris about his accident and approaches him on the wharf. Chris believes it is better to forget the past and in trying to evade her, falls off the pier into a boat and is knocked unconscious.

Chris is hospitalized. Lee tells the police that Ann badgered his brother and demands that she stay away from him.

Both Michael Rossi and Robert Morton instruct Ann to stay away from Chris because of the problems she's causing.

Already on probation for withholding facts about her past in her hospital job application, Ann disobeys Morton, enters Chris' room and begins questioning him. Morton overhears Chris shouting for Ann to leave and fires her. Ann plans on leaving Peyton Place but Michael admires Ann's determination to find the truth and persuades her to remain.

Chris finally confronts Lee with the fact that they both know Ann didn't push him off the bluff. What eventually comes out is that Lee was a sadistic, jealous and vengeful brother. He took Chris (age seven) up on Sailor's Bluff to play "blind man's bluff," because he knew Chris was scared of the cliff and fearful of falling. Chris refused to put on the blindfold. Then Ann Colby arrived, lonely and anxious to play, so they put it on her. Lee tormented her, throwing sticks, barking commands, and calling her names, abusing her the way he wanted to abuse Chris. Chris couldn't stand to watch what Lee was doing, so he went to pull the blindfold off of Ann. When he did, Lee pushed him over the edge. When Chris awoke on the rocks below he could hear all the kids screaming that Ann had done it because they were afraid of Lee.

Lee manages to convince Chris to maintain the family secrets, then continues to harass Ann.

At the Shoreline Garage, Steven threatens legal action against Lee if he continues to bother Ann. Lee tells Steven he should clean up his own backyard before looking in his (referring to Betty/Rodney).

Rodney arrives, Steven strides off and Rodney demands to know what Lee instigated. Lee turns on Rodney. He taunts him about his supposed affair with Betty then declares he's going to mess up Rodney's "pretty boy" face. Rodney fires Lee. Lee "decks" Rodney, and prepares to give him a beating. Rodney gets up and as the fight ensues, Lee's barroom brawling tactics are no match for Rodney's boxing skills. Rodney stands over a defeated Lee and commands him to get out.

Betty has walked out on Steven and her marriage in the heat of a bigger argument which stems from his unrelenting jealousy of Rodney. Although she hasn't given Steven reason to be jealous, Betty is forced to examine her own feelings for Rodney and Steven. She also knows he is the twin brother of Ann Howard and is afraid to tell him.

Steven reveals to Betty that he became a lawyer because he wanted power. He always envied Rodney and defended him so Martin Peyton and Leslie Harrington would need him. Betty listens patiently and asks for time.

Once Chris clears Ann of blame, Michael and Ann become engaged. However, his admission that Ann was not responsible triggers Lee's violent rage. After striking his brother, Lee supposedly goes looking for Ann.

A short time later, Allison discovers Ann's lifeless body at the foot of the bluff. She then sees Lee Webber riding his motorcycle along the summit and tossing away a bottle. Allison conveys this to Sgt. Goddard.

Michael Rossi is hungry for retribution. He finds Lee, accuses him of killing Ann, trying to kill Chris, then strikes him.

Lee is arrested on suspicion of murder in the death of Ann Howard. Lee instructs Sandy to find out what Allison told the police and to be sure to tell the police that he was with her (Sandy) when Ann fell. Sandy accuses Allison of lying to police, and Chris resents her, feeling she led him on.

Lee attempts to get Steven to defend him. He claims he didn't kill Ann. There is no real evidence against him and he believes Ann may have killed herself. Steven refuses but begins to think that Ann's death may have been the result of suicide instigated by his mother. Ann had been institutionalized because of her obsession with the bluff, then experienced a disastrous marriage. All of this left her somewhat unstable. Other factors create doubt as to Lee's guilt.

Leslie Harrington reveals that Hannah sought Ann hours before her death, and Rodney confirms he saw Hannah running from the mansion looking frightened. Steven decides to defend Lee and arranges for him to be let out on bail.

Allison, meanwhile, is deeply troubled by her discovery of Ann. Rodney is sympathetic and attempts to comfort her. He proposes marriage but Allison thinks he feels sorry for her.

Michael, who is also troubled, sees Allison standing on the bluff and brings her into his cottage. Allison almost collapses. Michael places her in the hospital and recommends to Constance that Allison see a psychiatrist in Boston.

Once Allison is left alone in her room at the hospital, she puts on her clothes and exits unseen. Steven and Betty (who have reconciled) see Allison wandering in the square near the bandstand.

Down on the wharf, Lee Webber accosts Allison and suggests she find somewhere to hide because he is out. Allison walks away, somewhat disoriented. She peeks in the window of the Shoreline Garage where she sees Rodney working and continues walking down the road north of the garage.

Lee's bail is revoked for approaching Allison (a potential witness in his murder case) on the wharf, and he is put back in jail.

Steven blames Hannah and Martin for maintaining their secret and resigns as Martin's attorney.

—END OF SEASON TWO—

Peyton Place
Season Three Summation
(September 12, 1966–September 11, 1967)

ALLISON MACKENZIE has disappeared without a trace. Elliot searches for his missing daughter in New York, but returns to Peyton Place unsuccessful.

A baby boy named Matthew is born to Constance and Elliot Carson which gives them hope and solace.

At Lee Webber's hearing, Michael Rossi testifies that he warned Lee to stop harassing Ann Howard, but that Lee was relentless. He also states that Constance Carson warned him that Lee was on a drunken spree after being fired by Rodney Harrington. However, Steven Cord cross-examines Michael and gets him to admit that he thought Ann (upset after her confrontation with Hannah Cord) might have leaped from Sailor's Bluff.

Chris Webber, who believes Lee is guilty, is subpoenaed by District Attorney John Fowler to testify against his brother.

Rodney Harrington and Sandy Webber who both feel lonely, are drawn together. Lee suspects their involvement and threatens Rodney when Sandy visits him in jail.

Rita and Norman Harrington go camping, and discover a teenage girl in an old abandoned log cabin. The girl behaves wild and is unwilling to talk. They chase her, a struggle ensues and the girl falls from a loft and is knocked unconscious. Rita and Norman discover that the girl has Allison's bracelet and they bring her back to town.

At the hospital, Michael Rossi tries to communicate with the girl who continues to be unreceptive. She bites Nurse Choate, throws a mirror and hairbrush at Rodney, and refuses to communicate with Elliot Carson.

Later, in Michael's office, during an examination, the girl reveals her identity. Her name is Rachel Welles, but she denies knowing Allison or anything about her.

A neighbor of Rachel's named Mrs. Burrows, arrives at the hospital and enlightens Michael Rossi about Rachel's background. Her parents (Mr. and Mrs. Welles) died in a fire. Since then, Rachel has been living with her mother's sister Lucy and her husband, Jack Chandler. However, Lucy recently died. Mrs. Burrows cautions that Jack Chandler will come for Rachel but she should not be allowed to go with him. Burrows feels he is a bad man.

Rachel leaves Doctor's Hospital fearful that she might be returned to the custody of her guardian, Jack Chandler. She's later caught hiding in the backroom of Eli Carson's general store by Rodney and Norman. Rodney wants to know about Allison and escorts Rachel to the police station.

While in custody, Rachel stabs herself and is returned to the hospital to be treated by Dr. Rossi. Rachel reveals that Jack Chandler married her Aunt Lucy to get her farm, and sometimes used a belt on Rachel as punishment. Michael promises her that she won't have to return to the farm with Chandler.

Rita and Norman befriend Rachel and Norman travels to Rachel's home town of Hastings Valley to find out more about her.

Meanwhile, Elliot Carson wants Steven Cord to pump Lee Webber for information on Allison, but Steven chooses to handle his client in his own way.

Martin Peyton makes a rare public appearance to testify for the prosecution in the preliminary hearing of Lee Webber. During the proceedings Peyton collapses and is taken to chambers. Michael Rossi uses a portable EKG unit to diagnose Peyton's condition but finds no abnormalities. Peyton returns to court and is cross-examined by Steven Cord at length. Steven oversteps his bounds, is called to chambers and dismissed by Judge Chester who adjourns court.

Jack Chandler arrives in town to claim Rachel and invades the sanctuary of the hospital. He ignore the rules and enters Rachel's room. Chandler explains that he will take Rachel back to Hastings Valley and both he and his sister Meg will take care of her. Nurse Choate summons Michael Rossi who tells Chandler to leave and stay away from Rachel. Chandler threatens to take Michael to court.

Rossi counters by threatening to take Chandler to court as an unfit guardian.

Constance visits Rachel in the hospital to gain information about Allison, but Rachel claims she has none. Elliot feels that Rachel knows something about Allison's disappearance, but her answers about Chandler are vague and evasive.

A meeting is arranged with Chandler at the police station. Rachel informs him she won't return with him to the farm and threatens to tell the police that she found Allison's bracelet on the floorboard of his car.

Hannah Cord testifies in court about her meeting with Ann Howard. It was the first time she had seen Ann since her birth. Ann was under the impression that Hannah was her mother; but Hannah discloses publicly that Catherine Peyton was the real mother of Steven Cord and Ann Howard. Both she and Martin Peyton concealed this fact for twenty-eight years.

Leslie Harrington reveals more related details to Rodney. Leslie eloped with Catherine because Martin Peyton had threatened to run him out of town if he came near his daughter. He wasn't good enough for a Peyton, and Catherine married him to spite her father. When the twins were born as a result of Catherine's affair with artist Brian Cord, Ann was given to her father who was paid to keep quiet. Hannah was hired by Peyton to be his housekeeper and Steven was given to her to be raised as her son. Leslie and Catherine lived in the mansion with Martin Peyton, Hanna (his housekeeper) and Steven. Catherine ignored

Steven and never acknowledged him as her son.

Rodney is critical of his grandfather for concealing the birth of two illegitimate children and using that information to manipulate their lives. Peyton replies he did so to protect his daughter, Rodney and Norman.

Judge Irwin Chester decides not to bind Lee Webber over for trial. John Fowler argues with Chester, claiming he made a serious mistake. Martin Peyton is outraged and vows to see Webber punished.

Before Hannah Cord leaves the mansion and Peyton Place, she torches the portrait of Catherine Peyton Harrington and a fire races through the interior of the Peyton house. Steven (who has come to the mansion to return the check that Hannah gave Betty for the sale of their house) finds Martin Peyton who has collapsed on the staircase, a victim of smoke inhalation and shock.

Peyton is treated at the hospital and regains consciousness.

Elliot Carson doesn't trust Rachel, yet despite his reservations, invites her to come and live with him and Constance who needs help with the baby. Rodney convinces Rachel that she should accept the offer and drives her to the Carson home.

Chris Webber is bursting with hatred for his brother. He's convinced that Lee murdered Ann Howard and feels Lee must be punished. He steals a gun from Ada Jack's tavern and plans to kill Lee. However, Lee finds the gun hidden in his living room sofa.

Sandy Webber confides in Chris that she cannot live with Lee any longer, and they discuss possibly leaving that very night, but first he plans to kill his brother (unknown to Sandy).

Chris arrives at the house, unlocks the door and shouts for Lee to make sure he's not there. He then prepares his trap by using two dining room chairs. He ties a string from the door knob to one chair 15 feet away, then ties another string from the knob to the other chair which he sits on. (The string is for aiming.) Chris cocks the gun, takes aim and prepares to shoot.

Lee is outside and aware that Chris is determined to kill him. He leaves and devises a plan to manipulate Steven Cord (who resents Lee, thinks he killed Ann Howard, and regrets having defended him) into the line of fire.

Lee tells Steven that Chris wants to commit suicide, believes Steven can reason with him, and gives him a key to the house.

Steven goes to the Webber home, unlocks the door and enters. Chris fires, nicking Steven's coat, and fires a second shot which misses him. Chris regrets missing his chance. Steven instructs him not to say anything more.

Sgt. Goddard arrives and questions Steven. Lee is brought in for questioning and claims that Chris threatened to kill himself.

After being interrogated by the police, Chris leaves for Boston, intending to travel on to California. Steven helps Chris onto the bus and makes a reservation for Sandy at the Colonial Post Inn.

Martin Peyton hires Betty to redecorate the mansion and agrees to allow Steven and Betty to move in after the renovations are completed. For Steven, it is a matter of accepting his birthright as a Peyton. He was never proud of being the child of a domestic.

Rodney in turn moves out and goes to live at the Shoreline Garage.

Martin Peyton returns to the mansion in a motorized wheelchair and is greeted by Steven and Betty who have moved in. Martin wants Betty to start running the household, paying bills, planning the menus, hiring and firing.

Michael Rossi returns from New York and is made Chief-of-Staff at Doctors Hospital.

Rita takes ill while making breakfast for Norman and is examined by Michael who believes she has a heart condition.

Rachel is accosted by Chandler when she returns to the Carson house with baby Matthew. Rachel becomes increasingly attracted to Michael who has given her a puppy, and acted as her protector. However, Michael feels too old for Rachel and explains they can only be friends.

Ada Jacks gives Sandy Webber (who plans to divorce Lee) Rita's old room at the tavern and advises her to put as much space between herself and Lee as possible.

Jack Chandler has decided to remain in Peyton Place to be near Rachel, but he needs a job. It happens that Chandler had some "shady dealings" with Leslie Harrington 20 years before in the back room of Ada Jack's Tavern. He approaches Leslie in his office and is given a job at the mill on the loading dock. The job comes with a stipulation that Chandler never phone Leslie or drops by his office again.

At the Tavern Ada recognizes Jack Chandler as Jack Forrest, a man that knew her husband Eddie Jacks and Leslie Harrington in the "old days." Ada is not fond of Forrest who asks to be called Chandler.

Rachel lies to Elliot Carson about being confronted by Jack Chandler on the wharf, further arousing Elliot's distrust and creating an argument between them. Rachel knows that Chandler has a connection with the Carson's missing daughter Allison. Yet if she reveals this explosive information, she and Carson face the potential violence of Jack Chandler. Rachel decides to leave the Carson home rather than being constantly questioned by Elliot, and she goes to stay with Rita and Norman.

Lee Webber applies for the job of Martin Peyton's chauffeur and gets hired. He is unaware that Martin has devious reasons for hiring him. Steven doesn't want Lee in the house. Ironically, Martin agrees with him but tells his grandson they will make their own justice.

Rachel, in an effort to help the Carsons, boards a bus and returns to Jack Chandler's farmhouse in Hastings Valley. She breaks in to look for clues that may shed light on Allison's disappearance. She finds a belt buckle with the initials "J.F." that may be a clue to Chandler's past. Rachel is then confronted by a surprise visitor, Jack Chandler. He informs her she won't be going back to Peyton Place. Rachel clobbers Chandler with a candlestick she's been carrying, and runs away. She's able to return to Peyton Place via a ride from her neighbor Mr. Burrows.

At the hospital Rachel seeks the aid and comfort of Michael Rossi who gives her a sleeping pill to get much needed rest. After she awakens, Elliot Carson apologizes for distrusting Rachel and encourages her to return to the Carson home.

On a dinner date with Sandy Webber who has filed for divorce, Rodney witnesses Lee manhandling her outside the Colonial Post Inn and hits him. Sandy wants more of a relationship with Rodney but he wants to maintain no-strings.

Jack Chandler returns to Peyton Place and steals Rachel's puppy. He sees a police car while walking in the square, so he quickly places the puppy in Peyton's limousine parked in front of the Clarion.

Lee Webber, who discovers the puppy, takes it back to the mansion where he now lives, and calls Rachel. He sees it as an opportunity to meet her and possibly get a date.

Rachel arrives at the mansion, receives the puppy and offers Lee reward money. He refuses and wants to take her out instead. Rachel tries to leave but Lee stops her with a forceful kiss. She tries to get away but he pursues and catches her. Betty comes in the front door and Rachel is able to elude Lee and leave.

Leslie Harrington is worried about the future of his sons and fearful that Martin Peyton may have disinherited Rodney and Norman. He pressures Betty to find out what is in the will by threatening to reveal the Blaine report (about her escapade in New York) to husband Steven.

Betty steals Peyton's will from the safe. Lee Webber sees her do it and reports it to Martin Peyton. The will leaves everything to Betty on the condition that she marry Rodney within one year of his death.

Lee Webber tells Steven that Betty took the will from Peyton's safe and about her visit to Leslie Harrington at the mill.

Elliot Carson has been investigating Jack Chandler and finds the belt buckle in Rachel's room. Elliot discovers the buckle was made in a Texas prison ten years before by a man named Jack Forrest imprisoned for assault. Elliot demands Rachel tell him everything about Chandler. She tells him that she found

Allison's bracelet in Chandler's truck and later found the buckle in his work clothes at the farm. Constance wants to call the police but Elliot decides to look for Chandler.

Rita, who is being treated by Michael Rossi for a heart condition, faints at Rodney's garage.

At the hospital Rossi prescribes two weeks of rest for Rita. Rita tells Norman she's stronger than Rossi thinks and really wants to have a baby.

Chandler confronts Leslie Harrington with the fact that Leslie wanted him to murder Elizabeth Carson, and on another occasion to get rid of Catherine. He insists that Leslie loan him $2,000 for a trip, and offers his farm as collateral. Leslie suggests he try the bank, then says he'll think it over.

Friction develops between Steven and Betty over her taking the will and lying to him about it. Martin Peyton asks Betty to return it, advises her to not steal anything that she wants, and to tell Steven the truth.

Elliot Carson has been looking for Jack Chandler, finds him on the wharf, and demands to know what happened to Allison. A fight ensues. Chandler throws a block at Elliot which misses, then Chandler swings an oar. Elliot takes it away from him and bangs Chandler against a post, ending the fight. Elliot again demands Chandler tell him where Allison is or he'll kill him. Chandler collapses.

The police question both Elliot and Chandler. Elliot dismisses the idea of filing a misdemeanor complaint, but Chandler claims Elliot jumped and assaulted him. Splinters matching an oar are found on Elliot's hands. Elliot explains that he took the oar away from Chandler. However, Elliot is arrested and faces one to twelve years in prison if convicted for felonious assault.

Steven represents him and Elliot is freed on bail.

Rachel visits a bruised and bandaged Chandler at the hospital, and pleads with him to leave the Carsons alone and leave Peyton Place.

Leslie fires Chandler from his job at the mill, gives him severance pay and offers him a huge amount of money to leave town. Chandler refuses it.

Martin Peyton summons Leslie to the park and wants him to help break up Betty and Steven's marriage. Martin is convinced that Betty is the kind of woman Rodney needs. Leslie is unhappy about Rodney working at the garage and very concerned about his future.

Peyton commissions artist Barrett Costa to do a portrait of Betty wearing Catherine Peyton Harrington's red dress. The portrait will cover the bare spot over the fireplace in the living room where Catherine's painting once hung. All of this is part of Peyton's master plan to pair off Rodney and Betty, to maintain a Peyton heritage that he thinks will do honor to his name.

Rodney visits the mansion and asks Martin for money to pay Rita's hospital bills. Norman is broke. Martin gives him the money. As Rodney leaves he encounters Betty in the red dress, and a quarrel ensues.

Rodney remarks that Betty is fortunate to no longer be his wife and now be married to Peyton's favorite grandson. Betty calls him a coward who never fights for anything he believes in. Rodney retorts that Betty is greedy. Betty runs up the stairs upset.

Steven receives an envelope from the Blaine detective agency in New York mailed at the request of Leslie Harrington. It contains their report on the alleged immoral activities of Betty Anderson during the time she spent in New York two years ago.

Michael Rossi arranges for Rachel to attend a girl's boarding school in Vermont. Rachel is very upset by the idea of leaving Peyton Place and wants to remain with Constance and Matthew.

Jack Chandler drops his charges against Elliot Carson, but Elliot knows that Chandler (a/k/a Jack Forrest) was imprisoned for assault and presses for Chandler's arrest. In the meantime, Chandler moves out of the boarding house where he's been staying, gasses up his car at the Shoreline Garage without paying, and drives off.

Elliot sees his last hope for the arrest and interrogation of Chandler collapse. Steven Cord, distracted by the Blaine report he received, failed to present the facts of Chandler's criminal past to the District Attorney's office, facts suggesting that Chandler might be involved in Allison's disappearance.

A birthday party for Steven is thrown by Martin Peyton at the mansion with several dignitaries in attendance, including the Lt. Governor and Judge Irwin Jessup. Steven arrives late and sees Rodney and Betty standing together. Peyton makes a toast to Steven, then the portrait of Betty is unveiled by the artist.

Peyton presents the portrait to Steven. Steven responds by giving a speech abut the blackmail contained in the Blaine report and accuses his grandfather of slandering his wife. He then hands it to Elliot to be printed in the Clarion. Betty runs upstairs humiliated by what has taken place. Rodney follows her and has a lengthy heart-to-heart conversation with Betty. He offers to get the Blaine report from Elliot and burn it. Betty admits she didn't love Steven when she married him, but her feelings have changed. Rodney feels he should have tried harder to keep himself and Betty together.

Rodney goes downstairs and assures Steven that nothing happened in New York. He encourages Steven to go upstairs and tell Betty that he believes her.

Betty explains to Steven what really took place in New York, as well as the conditions of the will which will make her the beneficiary. Once Betty confirms her love for him, Steven decides to fight the will and build a legal case against Peyton which would void the will.

Steven gets back the Blaine report from Elliot who had no intention of printing it. Elliot criticizes Steven's behavior at the party and urges him (as acting District Attorney) to get the police on Chandler's trail immediately.

Peyton invites Sandy Webber to the mansion and offers her $2,000 to leave town but Sandy throws the money back at him and leaves.

Steven and Betty leave the Colonial Post Inn after having

dinner and find Sandy in the back seat of their car. Sandy wants Steven to tell Rodney goodbye for her. She knows that she was in the way of Peyton's plan to break up their marriage. Sandy plans to go to California.

Rachel Welles has been permitted to attend night school as long as someone takes her and picks her up.

Chandler, hiding from the police, calls Rachel's school pretending to be Elliot, and learns when she'll be getting out. He then leaves an emergency message that Rachel will be picked up early and that she is to go outside and wait. Once she does, Chandler grabs and forces her into his panel truck. Deluded into thinking Rachel will accept him and go away with him, Chandler declares his love for her and plans to take her to Mexico where he'll buy a farm.

Enroute, when Chandler stops his truck at a railroad crossing, Rachel jumps out and escapes. Eventually she encounters Sgt. Goddard's police car and he returns her to the Carsons.

Elliot and Constance are determined to create an atmosphere of trust around Rachel which would allow her to divulge the truth about her relationship with Jack Chandler and her knowledge of Allison's disappearance. However, Elliot loses patience with Rachel in his quest for answers, and asks Michael Rossi to intercede. Michael too becomes frustrated and yells at Rachel.

Rachel carries out a desperate plan to regain the Carsons' love that she feels she lost through deception. She leaves the Carson house and takes Matthew. From a hospital linen closet, she calls Constance and tells her that Chandler took them, but Matthew is okay and she hangs up. Rachel then leaves Matthew at the hospital with a note. It explains that Chandler kept them prisoner but she made a deal to return the baby if she went away with him. The note ends with a goodbye and a thank you for everything.

Michael Rossi returns Matthew to the Carson home. Rachel meanwhile gets on an interstate bus leaving town but is picked up by the police and taken to the station. Jack Chandler is apprehended and placed in jail.

Rachel's plan has fallen apart and she's begun to decompensate. In an interview room she believes she is Allison and shows Michael and Steven Cord the bracelet that her father gave to her.

Michael decides to take Rachel to the state hospital for treatment. Before she is driven away, Rachel hands Allison's bracelet to Elliot and tells him to keep it for her.

In the Peyton County Courthouse, Leslie Harrington visits Jack Chandler in his cell. Chandler wants to be bailed out and threatens Leslie with exposure.

Leslie removes a revolver from his office at the mill and passes it to Chandler who uses it to escape. Norman witnesses the exchange and blackmails his father. His silence in return for the job vacated by Chandler that will help pay for Rita's medical bills.

Jack Chandler is later shot and killed by the police while trying to escape from a rooming house hundreds of miles from Peyton Place.

Adrienne Van Leyden, the beautiful young widow of Martin Peyton's former doctor, arrives at the mansion to be a house guest. In reality, Peyton has brought her there to break up Steven's marriage to Betty. Adrienne is the widow of the internationally renown research scientist Philip Van Leyden who fell from a high-rise apartment.

Michael Rossi who worked for Dr. Van Leyden on a research team, accuses Adrienne of killing her husband. He claims she changed him and caused his death.

Adrienne visit Steven Cord at his office under the guise of wanting to sue Michael Rossi for slander. Steven explains that slander is difficult to prove.

Betty finds out that Adrienne visited Steven and is upset that he didn't tell her. She feels he is punishing her because of the Blaine report. Steven responds that Adrienne is not his type.

Betty accuses Martin Peyton of using Adrienne Van Leyden as a means of breaking up her marriage. Peyton's countermove is to take Adrienne on a trip out of town. This momentarily blocks Steven Cord's efforts to subpoena Peyton's will as evidence of his mental incompetency.

Eddie Jacks (Ada's husband and Rita's father) returns to Peyton Place after an 18-year absence. Eddie, a con artist in debt, simply walked away from his family. During his absence he spent five years in prison. Ada never filed for divorce.

Peyton and Adrienne return to town. Peyton plans to underwrite a foundation in honor of Adrienne's husband. He offers Michael Rossi the position of running it, enabling him to do important research.

Rita is disturbed by Eddie's return and upset with Ada for not telling her he came back to Peyton Place. Ada had intended to make Eddie leave town.

Peyton continues to carry out his master plan to break up his grandson's marriage. Steven grows increasingly attracted to Adrienne and one afternoon they embrace on the beach.

Betty is informed by Lee Webber about Steven's encounter with Adrienne at the beach. Betty in turn confides to Rodney that she is losing Steven to another woman.

—END OF SEASON THREE—

Peyton Place
Season Four Summation
(September 15, 1967–September 19, 1968)

*E*DDIE JACKS GIVES RITA a savings bond and plans to leave town, but Rita offers to try and find him a job on the wharf. Ada Jacks reluctantly hires Eddie as a bartender for the night shift.

Betty moves out of the mansion into the Colonial Post Inn after seeing her husband and Adrienne Van Leyden leaving the Peyton mansion in Boston. Peyton recommends to Betty that she consult his lawyer about divorce proceedings and arranges an appointment for her.

Leslie Harrington opposes Martin Peyton's marriage to Adrienne Van Leyden for fear that Rodney and Norman would be cut out of the Peyton fortune. He enlists Eddie Jacks to get word to Peyton via Steven Cord about Adrienne's sordid past.

Adrienne has her suitcases packed, but Peyton proposes marriage and divulges an incriminating letter to dissuade Adrienne from leaving. However, Adrienne has tricked Peyton and unpacks her bags full of telephone directions.

Late at night Steven awakens Rodney at the Shoreline Garage and accuses him of knowing why Adrienne was brought to Peyton Place. A scuffle ensues and Rodney hits Steven.

Eddie Jacks carries out Leslie Harrington's request and informs Steven about Adrienne's background.

Norman's dislike and distrust of Eddie causes problems be-

165

tween Rita and him. During an argument between the two men, Eddie shoves Norman who cracks a rib.

Steven Cord plans to file incompetency charges against Martin Peyton, while Peyton urges Betty to change the grounds of her divorce from adultery to mental cruelty which appears better. Steven vows to fight the divorce and deposits money in his estranged wife's account to prevent her from taking money from Peyton. (Ultimately they sign a property settlement.)

At the competency hearing, Steven tries to impugn Adrienne's reputation but his tactics fail and the case is dismissed.

Leslie Harrington reaches a state of desperation and offers Eddie Jacks $50,000 to kill Martin Peyton before he can change his will.

Adrienne continually expresses her love for Steven. She begs him to save her from a loveless marriage, but Steven doesn't believe their relationship could work.

Peyton threatens to call off the wedding and furnish Phillip Van Leyden's letters, linking her to his death, unless Adrienne stops seeing Steven.

Leslie Harrington pressures Eddie Jacks to make his move, reminding him that there are only two days left until the wedding. Eddie removes a crescent wrench from the trunk of the Peyton limousine.

Adrienne attempts to steal the incriminating letters that link her to her former husband's demise, but she's caught by Peyton.

Peyton informs her that they'll be leaving Peyton Place. He has leased the apartment where Adrienne and her late husband lived. Adrienne is very upset by the idea.

Betty comes to the mansion that night and a confrontation ensues between her and Adrienne. At one point, Adrienne ascends the stairs to get away from Betty who follows. Adrienne turns around to hit Betty, loses her balance and plummets down the stairs. Betty checks to see if Adrienne is still alive, realizes she's dead and hurries off.

Eddie Jacks sees Betty leave the mansion, but doesn't recognize her before he slips in the back door. Martin Peyton hears a noise then calls for Lee Webber who is spending the night at the mansion. Lee grabs Eddie Jacks in the entry hall, and finds he has the wrench from the limo's toolbox. Peyton discovers Adrienne dead at the foot of the stairs. Lee orders Eddie to remove his right glove and makes sure Eddie gets his fingerprints on the wrench. Eddie claims that he came there to warn Peyton. Sgt. Ed Goddard and Sgt. William Walker arrive and take Eddie into custody.

Rita hears the police siren, looks out the apartment window and sees Eddie handcuffed and being taken into the police station. She runs out into the square and collapses. Norman carries her back into the apartment. He calls Dr. Rossi and Rita is taken to the hospital.

Eddie is charged with the murder of Adrienne Van Leyden. Eddie relates that he saw a dark-haired woman run from the mansion, and suddenly realizes it could be Betty.

It turns out Rita and her unborn child will be alright with rest, but Rossi advises Norman not to tell Rita about Eddie or Adrienne Van Leyden.

Martin visits Eddie Jacks in his cell once he believes that Eddie had no reason to kill Adrienne. Eddie tells Peyton he has the promissory note signed by Leslie Harrington for $50,000 to kill Peyton. Eddie adds he never intended to harm him.

Leslie visits Peyton at the mansion and denies knowing Eddie Jacks, although they're related through Rita.

Norman, who despises Eddie and blames him for Rita being hospitalized, promises his wife he'll help get Eddie out of jail. Norman asks his father for bail money. Leslie agrees to furnish the money with the stipulation that Eddie comes directly to him upon his release.

Martin promises Eddie $50,000 once he turns over the promissory note.

Martin knows Betty was with Adrienne before she died and presses her for the details. Betty reveals what happened and wants to go to the police. Martin encourages her not to. He'll protect her and Eddie Jacks will never go to trial.

Eddie and Leslie meet at the mill. Leslie wants the promissory note on his desk shortly after the bank opens on the next business day. He's unaware that Eddie betrayed him and sold the document to Martin Peyton.

Peyton activates his long-awaited plan to eliminate both Leslie Harrington and Lee Webber. He tells Leslie he is closing the mansion and leaving for Boston. He wants Leslie to take over the mill and all of his properties. His lawyer will meet Leslie at the mill that evening.

Peyton shows Lee Webber the promissory note that Eddie sold him. Leslie is waiting at his mill office for Peyton to sign over everything to him. Peyton instructs Lee to kill Leslie in return for whatever he wants. Lee agrees to do it and leaves. Peyton calls Leslie to warn him about Lee. He tells Leslie about the promissory note and will give Leslie everything he wants. In return, Peyton wants Leslie to kill the murderer of his granddaughter (Ann Howard). If not, Peyton threatens to go to the police.

Lee Webber enters Leslie's office and tells him that Peyton wants him to drive Leslie to the Inn for their meeting. Leslie turns his back and pulls out a gun before Lee can strike him with a nearby sports trophy. He turns and fires. Lee falls. Thinking Lee is dead, Leslie calls the police to report that he shot an intruder. Lee gets up, picks up the gun, points it at Leslie but doesn't fire. Instead he opens the door and leaves.

Lee, badly wounded, returns to the mansion realizing Peyton's true motives. He strikes Peyton with his own cane, then points the gun at him. Steven sneaks up behind Lee and jumps him. The gun goes off, Lee falls to the floor and dies.

Eddie Jacks gives Ada the bank deposit slip receipt for the $50,000 but is evasive as to where it came from. Steven visits the tavern and informs Eddie that Betty is indeed the "dark-haired woman" and that her confession to the police makes Eddie a "free man."

Martin Peyton's health is declining and he prepares to leave Peyton Place for the clinic in Boston. He leaves the mansion to Steven. In his farewell talk with Rodney, Peyton assures him it's important that Betty and he have found each other.

Peyton allows Leslie to continue managing the mill for the time being.

Michael Rossi receives an emergency phone call summoning him to the Cider Barrel on the wharf. A baby has taken ill aboard a bus passing through town and has been removed to the warmth of the nearest place.

The baby is transported to the hospital. Jill Smith arrives there and identifies herself as the mother of the sick baby. Michael Rossi explains to Jill that the baby has pneumonia and is in intensive care.

Jill takes a room at the Hewitt boarding house on the wharf with help from Eli Carson. Then she returns to the hospital to claim Kelly, her baby. Since Kelly has suffered from pneumonia and malnutrition, Michael Rossi is reluctant to sign over the release papers, but agrees to give Jill a second chance.

Eli Carson hires Jill to do "light chores" at his general store.

Constance, who had seen Jill in the square previously and mistook her for Allison, sees Jill a second time when she notices her peering through the window of the bookstore. She invites her in and forces Jill into a conversation, eager to know about her background. Jill reveals she has run away from home and hasn't seen her parents in more than a year. The baby has no father and Jill is looking for work.

Eddie visits Rita in the hospital. He candidly admits that he is leaving town because there doesn't seem to be enough room in her life for both Norman and him. As a result, Rita suffers an attack. Michael Rossi calls in a heart specialist to see if she needs surgery.

Rodney and Betty have gotten back together. When Rodney notices a bruise on Betty's cheek from a possible encounter with Steven, it leads to an angry confrontation and fist fight with his half-brother at the mansion. However, their fight is interrupted by an urgent phone call from Norman, summoning Rodney to the hospital due to Rita's condition.

Rita has suffered from a pulmonary edema. She was literally drowning in her own fluids. Her lungs had to be cleared before surgery to remove scar tissue from one of the principal passages to her heart. Rita successfully undergoes open heart surgery but suffers a miscarriage. Michael Rossi advises Norman that Rita will need a lot of rest and emotional support when she comes home.

Jill Smith who had previously sought legal advice from Steven Cord regarding custody, tells him that Kelly is Allison's baby. She asks if Steven will help her prove it. Steven visits Constance at the Book Gallery to find out if Allison was pregnant when she disappeared.

Elliot and Constance Carson question Jill about Kelly and Allison. Jill claims she named the baby. Michael Rossi, puzzled by her behavior, believes that Jill is the true mother and relates to the baby as any mother would.

Amidst all this, Joe Rossi, Michael's younger brother, arrives in Peyton Place unexpectedly. When Jill sees Joe in the square with his brother, she runs in the opposite direction. Joe doesn't admit to knowing Jill when asked about her.

Elliot and Constance consult Steven Cord. They want to try and obtain Kelly's birth certificate. Constance believes that if the child is Allison's, then Rodney is the father. Elliot begins to believe it and wonders if Rodney knew Allison was pregnant. Steven receives a telegram that states records certify that on the date in question, a baby girl was born to Allison MacKenzie.

Elliot Carson who blamed himself for Allison's disappearance now feels he has proof of the real reason Allison ran away.

Elliot goes to the Shoreline Garage and grabs Rodney. He tells him that Allison knew she was pregnant when she left town and shows him the telegram. Betty arrives. Elliot insists Rodney tell him the truth. Rodney admits he was totally involved with Allison but didn't know she was pregnant.

Jill doesn't wait for the paperwork and gives Kelly to Constance and Elliot.

Meanwhile, Joe Rossi tells Michael that he ran into a girl from home. Joe says that Jill claims the baby isn't hers. Joe asks Michael if Jill ever said anything to the doctor about Joe.

Rodney and Betty who have resumed their relationship are planning marriage, but the arrival of Kelly causes conflict between them. Betty has reservations about loving Allison's baby.

Rodney requests a paternity test but Rossi tells him he believes the baby is Jill's.

Constance examines the birth certificate and finds it odd that Allison listed her mother's maiden name as MacKenzie when it was Swain.

Rodney visits the Carsons to discuss the baby, but Elliot wants him to stay out of Kelly's life. Rodney confronts Jill as to why she never mentioned him and gave the baby to the Carsons.

Jill makes an urgent call to Steven Cord's office, concerned that Rodney wants custody of Kelly. While the birth certificate doesn't establish paternity, Steven makes Jill aware of how wealthy Rodney will be some day. Jill accuses Steven of using her as a client to create a conflict between Rodney and Betty, his former wife. Steven reminds her that Rodney has no chance of custody if he has no wife.

Norman has befriended Joe Rossi whom he works with at the Mill. However, when he brings Joe home for dinner, he reminds Rita of Joe Chernak and she begins to feel uncomfortable in his presence. Joe leaves.

Joe has been reluctant to tell his brother Michael what has forced him on the run. His hopes of Michael providing a safe haven has not worked out. A lot of unresolved resentment exists between them, stemming from their family history. Joe resents the fact that Michael left New York and feels he abandoned his family. Michael resents Joe for always demanding to be the center of attention in their household.

Norman Harrington agrees to drive Joe out of town, unaware as to why Joe is on the run.

Enroute to an intersection outside of town, Norman hits a curve too fast and the car turns over. Reverend Tom Winter, a Peyton Place resident for the past year, happens on the scene. He pulls both Norman and Joe out of the car and transports them to Doctors Hospital. Norman is treated and released, but Joe suffers a hairline fracture and remains in the hospital. He is later released in the care of Michael.

The custody hearing takes place and the Carsons get custody of Kelly. Michael thinks the Carsons have been taken in by Jill's lie and orders her to stay away from Constance and Elliot.

Michael suggests that Rita, who has been suffering emotionally, talk with Rev. Tom Winter.

Tom Winter tries unsuccessfully to help Rita gain some understanding of her recent depression, but promises to continue his efforts to help her. The Reverend has always been involved with the problems of others but has one of his own—his marriage. His wife Susan has always resented his going into the ministry. She feels neglected and questions his credential and right to help guide the lives of others. As a result of her troubled marriage, she drinks heavily.

Joe decides to confess to Michael about his past life and criminal involvement that forced him to run. He admits that Kelly is Jill's baby and his. He promised not to tell about the child because of his trouble in New York. Now he's through running.

Rita continues to battle her depression and experiences nightmares about her involvement with Joe Chernak. She confides in Tom Winter that she knew her baby wouldn't live because she shouldn't have married Norman. She loves him but must leave him. Tom emphasizes Norman's love for her and that Chernak is gone and powerless.

Eddie Jacks who is living in the same boarding house as Jill Smith, probes her about Joe Rossi's background. Eddie believes Joe is rotten and compares him to Joe Chernak.

Rita disappears from the apartment and no one knows where she had gone. Eddie barges into the Cider Barrel where

Joe Rossi is eating, grabs him and demands to know where Rita is. He gets no satisfaction and leaves.

A short time later, Joe sees Rita. Aware that people are looking for her, Joe follows Rita into a warehouse on the wharf. Rita has returned to that disturbing moment when she first met Joe Chernak. Once inside she experiences a flashback. Joe goes inside, tries to help and explains that he is not Joe Chernak.

Eddie Jacks, who has been searching for Rita, enters the warehouse, sees his daughter is hysterical, and attacks Joe. Joe is able to fend off Eddie and escape, but Eddie pursues him and continues his assault. Finally, Joe "decks" Eddie with a hard right in self-defense. Joe calls Michael to come right away.

Ada and Rita help Eddie into the back room at the tavern. Rita tells Ada the fight was her fault. She went to the warehouse to relive the past, to try and overcome it.

Michael Rossi treats Eddie for a forehead wound, and admonishes Joe.

At that point, Joe Rossi decides to "clear the air" once and for all. He goes to the beach house and gets a photograph of Allison that he brought from New York. It was given to his sister by Michael during his trip to New York the year before. Joe goes to the Carsons and tells them that Jill and he are the parents of Kelly. Jill used Allison's name on the birth certificate after seeing her photo and learning about her.

Eddie Jacks wants to go to the police about what happened but Rita explains that Joe never touched her. A short time later when Rita returns to the tavern, she learns that her father has left Peyton Place. In a farewell note, Eddie explains that he wanted to help Rita but wound up hurting her. It appears he got started too late with her and her mother. He advises Rita to place all her faith and trust in Norman who has the qualities to make her happy.

Kelly is given back to Jill, and Joe is ordered by the Court to pay for child support.

In an effort to help Jill and Kelly, Michael Rossi arranges for her to meet Tom Winter regarding a secretarial job.

Elliot Carson is offered a job doing editorials and special assignments at a newspaper out of town. Both Elliot and Constance agree that they should get away from the daily reminders of a troubled past. They decide to leave Peyton Place.

Eli Carson and Michael Rossi agree to fix up the Carson house, then either rent or sell it.

William Kennerly, Jr. (Martin Peyton's lawyer) arrives at the Colonial Inn and informs Leslie Harrington that the Peyton Mill has been sold and that Leslie is dismissed.

Friction develops between Joe Rossi and Tom Winter over Jill Smith. Joe, who still has feelings for Jill despite their differences, is jealous after continually seeing Jill and Tom together.

Betty and Rodney are married by Tom Winter. Steven Cord is embittered by their marriage and admits to Susan Winter that he will never give up his claim to Betty. Susan shares similar feelings with regard to her husband. Faced with a disintegrating marriage, she plans to drive her husband to admit he is a man before he is a minister. Susan decides to put Tom's human frailty to the test by moving secretary Jill into their home.

Ada Jacks gives Norman and Rita the $50,000 bank receipt from Eddie. He wanted to make sure Rita's future was secure.

The Carson home is rented on a short term lease by Marsha Russell, an attractive divorcee and her seventeen year old daughter Carolyn. Carolyn Russell is a pretty girl with a sharp wit, dry sense of humor and a maturity beyond her years, yet she feels like a child triggered by restraints imposed by her protective mother. Carolyn is also confused and bitter about he parents' divorce.

Carolyn meets Joe Rossi at the Founders Festival and is intrigued by his being a bit "rough around the edges." She puts him on, yet Joe challenges her and she runs off. Joe later takes Carolyn out on a date, but when he "comes on" to her, she evades him.

Marsha Russell disapproves of Joe and complains to Michael that Joe is forcing himself on Carolyn. She asks him to keep his brother away from her daughter whom she feels is a sweet, innocent and attractive teenager.

Joe agrees not to ask Carolyn Russell out again, realizing they are two very different people, and that she is not really interested in him. However, Joe is left unsettled. He has never been able to accept that Jill, the mother of his child, has refused to have anything to do with him. He's waited patiently, hoping she might have a change of heart, but that hasn't happened.

Carolyn begins seeing Jeff Kramer, a high school friend who plays keyboard in a group called the Pillory Rock Band.

Marsha Russell begins to date Michael Rossi.

Norman and Rodney go into partnership and open Harrington Brothers Motorcycles Inc. at Rodney's garage. Norman uses the money from Eddie Jacks that indirectly came from their grandfather.

Tom Winter, working in close quarters with Jill Smith on a daily basis, begins to develop feelings for her. Jill begins to feel trapped and uncomfortable in the Winter home. Jill confronts Tom with regard to his feelings. His denial of those feelings becomes an admission Tom is confused and Jill offers to leave.

During a meeting in Boston between Steven and Peyton's lawyer William Kennerly, Jr., the $50,000 promissory note (that Peyton promised to Eddie Jacks) is mentioned and Steven later steals the paper which has a notation of the $50,000 deal.

Steven returns to Peyton Place and seeks out Betty at the motorcycle shop. He tells her about the $50,000 contract he learned about in Boston. Steven persuades Betty to take a ride with him while he enlightens her further.

Outside of town, Rodney and Norman are trying out a motorcycle (Rodney is driving with Norman on the back). They swerve to avoid hitting Steven's car and the bike crashes into a tree.

Norman escapes injury, but as a result of the accident, Rodney is paralyzed from a spinal cord injury and unable to move his arms or legs. Emergency surgery is performed which saves Rodney's life, but he remains paralyzed.

Tom Winter's desire for Jill Smith intensifies while Susan Winter continues drinking. Jill leaves the Winter's home after Tom grabs and kisses her. Susan seems to have accomplished her goal to convince Tom he is not worthy of serving God. Jill has apparently rejected him and perhaps now he will turn to her.

Tom searches for Jill, knowing his uncontrollable feelings caused her to leave his home. When they meet Tom feels they need each other, but Jill doesn't love Tom, feels his wife needs him, and asks Tom to leave her alone.

Rodney begins to regain some sensation and Dr. Harry Miles (a neurosurgeon who has been treating Rodney) tells Betty and Norman that Rodney will make it back on his feet.

Steven visits Rodney and tries to explain why Betty was with him in the car when the accident occurred. Rodney tells him to get out. Betty angrily accuses Steven of "poisoning" Rodney's mind with the impression that they were on a joy ride.

Tom Winter travels to Boston and resigns from the ministry while Susan is admitted to the hospital to "dry out."

Jill's baby is taken away from her by Child Welfare Services until Judge Chester makes a decision about custody.

Rita and Norman are awarded custody of Kelly until Jill can provide a "suitable atmosphere to raise the child."

Michael Rossi who advocated for Jill in court wants her to work as a nurse's aide and offers to advance her a month's rent for a room at the boarding house.

Rodney Harrington is given a new therapist names Chuck Atwill who pushes him to get better.

—END OF SEASON FOUR—

Peyton Place
Season Five Summation
(September 23, 1968–June 2, 1969)

*T*OM WINTER INSTRUCTS Steven Cord to file for a divorce from Susan, then gets a job on a fishing boat.

Fred Russell drives down from Boston to visit Carolyn and admits that his affair with another woman was the cause of his divorce from Marsha.

Joe Rossi begins to accept the responsibility of fatherhood. He visits with Rita ad Norman to spend more time with Kelly, and wants to work out a time schedule. Dissension still exists between Jill and him.

Steven Cord, feeling guilty about his part in Rodney's accident, donates therapy equipment to the hospital but does it anonymously.

Carolyn Russell, still hurt and confused by her parents' divorce, sees Marsha's relationship with Michael Rossi as a betrayal. Marsha fears she might lose her daughter and feels she should stop seeing Michael.

Harry and Alma Miles' 18-year-old son Lewis arrives in Peyton Place after spending time in New York.

Rodney Harrington's recovery is plagued by nagging doubts about Betty's loyalty. (She was in the car with Steven when the accident occurred.) These concerns have placed him in a state of despair and hampered his effort to recover.

Joe Rossi decides that it is best for him to leave Peyton

Place. However, when Jill Smith finds out, they reconcile and plan to get married. Jill and Joe are given custody of Kelly and they leave town.

Susan Winter who still loves Tom, makes herself available to Steven who at first isn't interested but begins to respond to her out of need.

Martin Peyton dies at the Boston Clinic. Betty Harrington, the principal beneficiary of Peyton's will now has vast wealth and patronage.

Slowly the sensation and feeling has returned to Rodney's body along with some of his motor skills. Michael Rossi and Harry Miles both agree to allow Rodney to return home to the converted barn-house near the wharf that he shares with Betty. Chuck Atwell will continue to pick Rodney up every day and bring him to the hospital for therapy.

Marsha Russell is concerned about Carolyn's involvement with Jeff Kramer and asks Fred for help in dealing with her. Once Fred returns to town, he learns from Jeff that he is having a casual relationship with Carolyn. Fred tells Jeff to stay away from his daughter.

Betty, with her newly-acquired wealth, wants to buy the mansion from Steven who refuses to sell. Susan informs Betty she plans to marry Steven and live with him in the mansion.

Carolyn visits Fred in Boston and is surprised to find his mistress Donna Franklin in his apartment

Marshal Russell has resumed seeing Michael Rossi, and agrees to marry him.

Lew Miles calls a New York hospital, identifies himself as Dr. Harry Miles and inquires about a male patients named E.J. Cunningham who is in a coma.

Harry becomes angry with Lew when he receives a strange and disturbing phone call from a girl in New York. Harry is now convinced that Lew is in serious trouble and has lied to him.

Seventeen-year-old Vicki Fletcher arrives in Peyton Place to get a fresh start with a specific person—Lew Miles. Lew is surprised by her arrival but asks Alma if she can stay at the Miles home in his older brother Cliff's room. (Cliff is away in the military.)

Harry Miles learns that Vicki is pregnant. Both he and Alma are concerned because Vicki and Lewis are so young. Harry remains suspicious of Lew's activities in New York and decides to go there and find out what happened.

Betty Harrington offers Steven Cord twice the market value for the Peyton mansion and Steven agrees to sell. However, the bank informs him that Betty's check has no value. Betty and Steven make a hurried trip to Boston to investigate the finances of his late grandfather. Attorney Wainwright explains to them that everything has been left to the Peyton Foundation and denies them access to the revised will. Betty is now the beneficiary of nothing. Steven and Betty vow to fight the will.

Rodney begins to move his arms and legs once again, and prepares to go home. However, he wants time and space to resolve his marital conflicts. Betty moves out of their barn-house, allowing Rodney to get the separation needed.

Carolyn Russell encounters Jeff Kramer on the street. They begin to argue, she breaks free and runs away. Fred Russell appears, grabs Jeff and hits him. Jeff explains they were arguing about Lew Miles.

Fred drops in at the Russell home to confront Carolyn about what Jeff Kramer told him regarding Lew Miles.

Carolyn in turn confronts Jeff at the Shoreline Café, accusing him of lying to her father abut Lew and her.

Carolyn and Lewis agree on a way to handle the false rumors that have linked them together. However, their agreement is reached in full view of Fred Russell.

Fred insists that Carolyn not be seen with Lewis Miles again. This starts another argument. Carolyn antagonizes her father by telling him that Marsha is planning to marry Michael Rossi and there is nothing he can do about it.

Rodney arrives home having planned to go to college in Boston and study to be a teacher. Rita and Norman come over and help him pack.

Rodney shows Betty a letter to a Boston real estate firm asking them to find an apartment large enough for two people. Rodney intends to make it without the inheritance. Betty feels their marriage will work this time. Norman, Rita, Rodney and Betty drive off to Boston.

Rodney gets an apartment on the river near campus and Betty travels back and forth to be with him.

Betty puts their house up for sale and decides not to protest the Peyton will. Steven Cord will go it alone.

Jennifer Ivers, one of Peyton's nurses, offers Betty and Steven a deal. She is willing to testify that Peyton was mentally unstable. However, Steven discovers that Hanna Cord may have put Ivers up to it and his interest wanes. Betty also chooses to move on.

Fred Russell begins to lose control. He warns Dr. Harry Miles if he wants to remain at Doctors Hospital to make sure that people don't start talking abut his son Lewis and the way he (Harry) encourages him to pursue a "white girl."

Meanwhile Marsha Russell and Michael Rossi plan to drive across the state line and get married.

Carolyn and Jeff are walking to the hospital, followed by Lewis and another girl when Fred approaches Lew and stats an argument. Michael Rossi intercedes. Fred warns him to stay out of it. Both men argue and almost come to blows. Norman Harrington arrives to break it up.

Marshal and Michael hope that their upcoming marriage will force Fred to stop his harassment of them and Carolyn. However, Fred refuses to accept the new situation.

On the night of Marsha and Michael's planned elopement, Fred invades Marsha's home and molests her. Fortunately, Jeff Kramer arrives at the house and Marsha is able to get Fred out the door.

Once Michael Rossi learns what happened, he goes after Fred, finding him in his room at the Colonial Post Inn.

Marsha and Sgt. William Walker arrive at the Inn and find Michael trying to revive an unconscious Fred. Michael explains that Fred had too much to drink and apparently keeled over before he got there.

Michael calls for an ambulance. Fred is transported to the hospital where it's discovered that Fred has a severe head injury. At one point he regains consciousness and tells Marsha that Michael Rossi is responsible for his injury.

Fred dies a short time later and Michael is booked on suspicion of murder. Bail is denied.

Sgt. Walker informs Lew Miles that he has an arrest warrant for him for a felony hit-and-run in New York. Lew declares he is through running and ready to accept responsibility. Harry and Alma vow to support Lew and allow him to make his own decisions in the future.

Tom and Susan Winter meet and on a note of closure, Susan agrees to see Dr. Rossi about her problem.

Eli Carson proposes marriage to Maggie Riggs, his elderly companion, and she accepts.

At Michael Rossi's preliminary hearing, Marsha Russell testifies about Fred's abuse, but admits that Fred accused Michael of causing his injury. Norman testifies about the incident between Fred and Michael where they almost came to blows. Ada Jacks relates a negative incident that occurred between the two men at the tavern. As a result, Michael is bound over for trial and led away to his jail cell.

—END OF SEASON FIVE—

SHOOTING FINAL
January 25, 1968

PEYTON PLACE

EPISODE No. 427

EXECUTIVE PRODUCER
PAUL MONASH

PRODUCER
EVERETT CHAMBERS

AIR DATE
APRIL 25, 1968

TWENTIETH CENTURY-FOX TELEVISION, INC.

Sample Teleplay
Episode #427

THE FOLLOWING is an eight page example of a final shooting script from the fourth season completed January 25th, 1968. It aired three months later on April 25th, 1968.

At this point in the storyline, Rita Harrington (Patricia Morrow), who underwent open-heart surgery and experienced a miscarriage, has been battling depression and experiencing nightmares about her involvement with the late Joe Chernak (killed in a fight with Rodney Harrington almost three years before). Norman Harrington has befriended Joe Rossi (Michael Christian), but Rita is uncomfortable around Joe because he reminds her of Joe Chernak. Eddie Jacks (Dan Duryea) believes Joe to be rotten and has it in for him. When Rita disappears from her apartment, Eddie believes Joe is involved and demands to know where his daughter is. However, Eddie gets no satisfaction because in reality, Joe has nothing to do with Rita's disappearance.

After his confrontation with Eddie, Joe sees Rita going into a warehouse by the wharf. He follows, knowing Rita's family is searching for her, very concerned about her disappearance.

"PEYTON PLACE"

EPISODE #427

FADE IN

EXT. WHARF - HIGH ANGLE - NIGHT   159

To see a distraught RITA move OUT of the shadows of the
Boat Rental shack area, looking quickly toward the Tavern,
wanting to avoid being seen, as:

> NARRATION
> Rita Harrington has come back...
> back to that terrifying moment in
> her life when she first met the
> late Joe Chernak.

Rita continues on past the Shoreline Garage toward the
warehouse, as:

> NARRATION
> Back to a warehouse on the
> Peyton Place wharf where, in the
> shadows, she accepted a way of
> life that has tormented her ever
> since.

She ENTERS the warehouse.

INT. WAREHOUSE - HIGH ANGLE - NIGHT   A-159

Dark. Deserted. Then, the SOUND of a heavy door opening,
a splash of light from outside, and a slender figure
slipping inside. CAMERA DROPS, TIGHTENS, as Rita leans
against the door, winded, sobbing lightly. Moment. Then,
regaining her composure, she lifts her eyes, surveys the
surroundings, and starts forward INTO the darkness with
an air of resolution.

ANOTHER ANGLE   B-159

as Rita moves slowly down a corridor of crates, seemingly
braced for an encounter. CARRY her around a corner, then
she stops, turns slowly, forces herself to look at an open
area adjacent to a large work table. Visibly shaken by
the surroundings, she reaches back for an extra ounce of
control. Finding it, her features begin to relax, but
suddenly she starts at a sharp, metallic SOUND. Her head
jerks toward the door as her hand goes to her mouth
stifling the urge to cry out, and she tries hard to listen
above the pounding of her heart. Silence. Then she
glances back at the spectre-like shapes in the area she
came to face, and begins a slow retreat.

                                                    Cont.

CAMERA MOVES with her back into the corridor. Her pace
quickens as she nears the last stack of boxes before the
door, then reaching it, she stops suddenly. A FIGURE
LOOMS in her path, engulfed in shadow, unidentifiable --
except to Rita:

                   RITA
            (thinly)
   Joe...

There is no reply. Rita shakes her head as if wishing
the apparition away.

                   RITA
            (louder)
   Joe Chernak...

And as the figure takes a half-step forward, Rita can no
longer suppress an ear-shattering SCREAM. TIGHT on her
terror-filled face, then:

ANGLE PAST JOE TO RITA   C-159

JOE'S back is to the CAMERA as we see Rita half-run, half-
fall backwards in an attempt to get away. CAMERA FOLLOWS
HER as she scurries away from Joe.

                   RITA
   No! No!

Joe moves past the CAMERA toward her.

                   JOE
            (tightly)
   Shut up, will you?

NEW ANGLE - RITA   160

as she trips and falls down on the warehouse floor. Joe's
hand comes INTO the SHOT as he grabs her wrist (to help
her up) but she jerks away from him.

CAMERA MOVES IN TIGHT on Rita's terror-filled face, as
Joe's hand slams down over Rita's mouth; she struggles.

NEW ANGLE - JOE AND RITA   161

as she struggles to get free, to get his hand off her
mouth, but she's unable to; after a moment she goes limp,
her eyes closed. He removes his hand quickly, now:

                                                                     Cont.

                    JOE
               (urgently)
     I'm not Joe Chernak, Rita. You
     understand? I never even knew
     Joe Chernak, and anyway he's dead,
     understand? I'm Joe Rossi.

He looks at her, her eyes are closed.

                    JOE
     Look at me, Rita.

He helps her to sit up.

NEW ANGLE - RITA   162

as she resists for a moment and then sits up; her eyes
still tightly closed.

                    JOE
               (gently)
     Come on, Rita. I'm not Joe Chernak.

Now she opens her eyes, stares up into his face.

                    JOE
     I don't want to have to hide
     every time I see you coming.
               (beat)
     I'm not Joe Chernak. See?

She nods. The tension released, Rita breaks down, starts
to cry softly.

                    JOE
     I'm sorry I had to put my hand
     over your mouth, but...

She tries to get up but she suddenly feels too weak; her
face goes white as she starts to lean toward him. She
can't stop sobbing.

                    JOE
     Hey. Take it easy.

                    RITA
     I'm so...dizzy.

She sags against him, half-fainting; concerned, he keeps
her propped up for a moment as he moves a crate out from
behind her.

                                                  Cont.

                    JOE
            You just lie down for a few
            minutes until you feel better.

NEW ANGLE - JOE AND RITA   163

Joe's back is to us now as he carefully helps Rita lie
back on the warehouse floor. Suddenly EDDIE JACKS moves
PAST the CAMERA and grabs a startled Joe by the shoulders
and lifts-pulls him off the floor and away from Rita and
slams him against the wall.

Joe now sees that it's a half-crazed looking Eddie who
has grabbed him.

                    JOE
            Listen, you...

Eddie lunges at Joe's throat. Joe manages to shake Eddie
off.

                    JOE
            Rita started screaming. She
            thought I was Joe Chernak.

Eddie lunges at Joe again, this time knocking Joe down.

                    JOE
            Get off me... All I tried to
            do was...

Eddie swings a right at Joe; Joe ducks but gets caught
on the side of the head, slowing him down long enough for
Eddie to get to his feet and grab a hunk of pipe. Joe
gets up, just in time to see it coming; he moves aside
and knocks Eddie off-balance.

                    JOE
                 (tightly)
            I don't want to fight you.

Joe grabs the pipe out of Eddie's hand and flings it o.s.

CLOSE ON RITA   164

Horrified by Eddie's unprovoked attack, she struggles to
her feet, moves toward the two men.

ANGLE PAST JOE TO EDDIE   165

Eddie throws a wooden crate at Joe; it BANGS into the wall
narrowly missing him. Joe pushes a crate between them.

                                                    Cont.

                    JOE
               (angrily)
          I'm not going to be your
          punching bag, old man.

Eddie kicks the crate out of the way but is stopped by
Rita as she moves INTO the SHOT and grabs his arm.

                    RITA
          He didn't do anything. Dad,
          stop it.

We see Joe takes advantage of the interruption to run for
it. He moves OUT of SHOT over:

                    RITA
          Leave him alone.

We HEAR the DOOR SLAM SHUT o.s., just as Eddie shakes
loose of Rita and moves OUT of the SHOT after Joe. Rita
goes after her father.

EXT. WHARF - LONG SHOT - AREA IN FRONT OF TAVERN - NIGHT 166

as Joe runs, then slows to a walk toward CAMERA; after a
moment he looks back over his shoulder and sees Eddie
coming after him. (NOTE: If possible, this should be in
the area of Joe Chernak's death).

                    RITA'S VOICE
               (o.s. through tears)
          Leave him alone, please, Eddie.

For a moment Joe hesitates, then he turns and keeps on
walking away from Eddie; now we see Eddie start running
toward Joe. Joe turns around, sees Eddie coming at him
again, calls out.

                    JOE
          Lay off, old man - I'm warning
          you!

Eddie comes on, tries to grab Joe in a hammer lock.

                    RITA
               (approaching them)
          Stop it! Stop it! Both of
          you!

                                             Cont.

In a flash, Joe breaks loose, hits Eddie with a left in
the gut and as Eddie doubles over, Joe bends him backwards
and lays him out with a hard right to the side of the head.
Rita SCREAMS as she sees her father go down.

Joe bends over Eddie, who lies, motionless, on the ground;
his face is cut and bleeding slightly. Rita kneels down
beside Eddie.

                    JOE
      I told him... I didn't want to
      fight him. I told him...

ANGLE PAST RITA AND JOE TO TAVERN ENTRANCE   167

First we see a COUPLE OF CUSTOMERS come OUT of the Tavern
to see what's going on. ADA rushes OUT. Rita holds her
father's head in her lap. One Customer DISAPPEARS inside
the Tavern.

NEW ANGLE - RITA AND JOE   168

as Joe starts backing away, alarmed now, he collides with
Ada, who stands staring down at Eddie's unconscious form.

                    ADA
      (almost a whisper
      to Joe)
  Why'd you hit him like that, Joe?

As Ada stares down at the prostrate Eddie, and the sobbing
Rita, Joe moves away, then turns and runs. We see
SEVERAL MEN and WOMEN from the Wharf and Tavern gather
around Eddie and Rita, and the shocked Ada.

ANOTHER ANGLE - AT PHONE BOOTH   169

As Joe slams inside the phone booth, frantically drops in
a coin, dials, stares outside at the fallen Eddie. A
moment, then:

                  ROSSI'S VOICE
    (o.s.)
  Dr. Rossi...

                  JOE
  Mike...

INT. ROSSI'S HOUSE - NIGHT   170

ROSSI is on the phone.

                            INTERCUT:

JOE AND ROSSI ON PHONE   A-170

>   ROSSI
> Joe. What is it?
>
>   JOE
> You got to get down to the Wharf
> right away. With your black bag.
> It's Eddie Jacks. He's hurt.
>
>   ROSSI
>   (ice-cold
>   contempt)
> You mean you picked a fight --
> with a man three times your age?
>
>   JOE
> He started it. I had to slug him,
> or he'd have killed me.

Rossi, tight-lipped, goes to get his medical kit, over:

>   ROSSI
> How hard did you 'slug' him?
>
>   JOE
>   (a beat, then)
> He's out - cold. I didn't start
> it, Mike.
>
>   ROSSI
> Sure, sure. Where is he?
>
>   JOE
> Right out in front of the Tavern.
>
>   ROSSI
> Stretched out.
>
>   JOE
> Yeah.
>
>   ROSSI
> Don't move him. I'll be right
> down.
>
>   JOE
> Rita saw the whole thing and
> she'll tell you he was in the
> wrong, not me.

                                                      Cont.

                    ROSSI
              (bitterly)
          That's the way it always is,
          isn't it, Joe? The other guy's
          always in the wrong?
              (beat)
          See you.

He hangs up. Joe hangs up, a wave of anger coming over him. Furious at Rossi, he moves OUT of the booth, viciously slams the booth door. The crack of the SOUND turns him quickly to the small group hovering over Eddie.

ANOTHER ANGLE - PAST THE FALLEN EDDIE TO JOE   171

Ada and Rita have turned at the SOUND of the door on the booth; they stare at Joe. Slowly, he moves to join them.

                                              FADE OUT

                    FIRST COMMERCIAL

Production Staff

Executive Producer	Paul Monash
Producer	Everett Chambers (1965–1969)
	Richard Goldstone (1964–1965)
Line Producer	Felix Feist (1965)
Associate Producers	William Hole Jr.
	Lloyd Rosamond (1964)
	Therese Lewis (1964)
Executive Script Consultant	Richard De Roy (1964–1968)
Script Consultant	Steven Carabatsos (1964)
Story Editors	Nina Laemmle (1964–1969)
	Del Reisman (1965–1969)
Directors	Walter Doniger (1964–1968)
	Ted Post (1964–1969)
	John Newland (1965)
	Jeffrey Hayden (1965–1966)
	Harvey Hart (1966–1968)
	Lee Phillips (1966–1969)
	John Erman (1967–1969)
	William Hole Jr. (1967–1968)

Director of Photography	Robert Hauser A.S.C.
	Dale Deverman A.S.C.
	William Cronjager A.S.C.
Camera Operator	Robert Sparks
	William Cronjager
Assistant Cameramen	Randall Robinson
	Tom Del Ruth
Writers	Sonya Roberts
	Lionel Siegel
	Michael Gleason
	Carol Sobieski
	John Wilder
	Jerry Ziegman
	Rita Lakin
	Peggy Shaw
	Ann Marcus
	Mal Marmorstein
	Richard Carr
	Lee Erwin
	Robert J. Shaw
	Theodore & Mathilde Ferro
	Kenneth Hartman
	Sam Washington
	Wharton Jones
	Mark Saha
	Gene Boland
	Don Balluck
	Franklin Barton
	Laurence Richards
	Jessica Stephans
	James Griffith
	Jerry Thomas
	Miriam Rosamond
Production Manager	Gaston Glass

Production Staff

Art Directors	Jack Martin Smith
	Jack Senter
	Stan Johnson
Set Decoration	Walter M. Scott
	William Calvert
	Robert de Vestel
Music	Fred Steiner
	Arthur Morton
	Cyril Mockridge
Theme	Franz Waxman
Music Conducted & Supervised by	Lionel Newman
Supervising Music Editor	Leonard Engel
Music Editor	Kenneth Hall
Film Editors	Jamie Caylor
	Basil Wrangell
	Chuck McClelland
Sound Effects Editor	Ralph Hickey
	Jack Kirschner
Post Production Coordinator	Robert Mintz
Assistant Directors	Wilbur McGaugh
	William Allyn
	William Sheehan
	Jack Gertsman
	Steven Bernhardt
	Lynn Guthrie
Post Production Supervisor	Dan Nathan
Property Master	James Parrish
Casting	Joe Scully
Assistant to Executive Producer	Ceil Armanda

The Daytime Series

Return to Peyton Place
(NBC 1972–1974)
DAYTIME DRAMA

Executive Producer	Don Wallace
Producer	George Paris
Associate Producer	Gail Kobe
Head Writer	James Lipton
Writer	Jim Bullock
Directors	Frank Pacelli, Alan Pultz

CAST

Constance MacKenzie	Bettye Ackerman (1972)
	Susan Brown (1972–1974)
Allison MacKenzie	Katherine Glass (1972)
	Pamela Susan Shoop (1972–1974)
Dr. Michael Rossi	Guy Stockwell
Elliot Carson	Warren Stevens
Betty Anderson	Julie Parrish (1972–1973)
	Lynn Loring (1973–1974)

Rodney Harrington	Lawrence Casey (1972)
	Yale Summers (1972–1974)
Norman Harrington	Ron Russell
Steven Cord	Joseph Gallison
Leslie Harrington	Frank Maxwell (1972)
	Stacy Harris (1972-1974)
Selena Cross Rossi	Margaret Mason
Martin Peyton	John Hoyt
Rita Harrington	Patricia Morrow
Eli Carson	Frank Ferguson
Ada Jacks	Evelyn Scott
Mathew Carson	John Levin

The Two Network TV Movies

Murder in Peyton Place
(NBC October 3, 1977)
Twentieth Century Fox Television
Peter Katz Productions
Produced by: Peter Katz
Written by: Richard DeRoy
Directed by: Bruce Kessler

Stella Chernak secretly returns to Peyton Place to exact revenge for an incident that occurred 12 years before.

--- CAST ---

Constance Carson	Dorothy Malone
Dr. Michael Rossi	Ed Nelson
Elliot Carson	Tim O'Connor
Norman Harrington	Christopher Connelly
Jill Harrington	Joyce Jillson
Betty Anderson	Janet Margolin
Steven Cord	David Hedison
Stella Chernak	Stella Stevens
Ellen Considine	Marj Dusay

Stan Haley	Jonathan Goldsmith
Denise Haley	Charlotte Stewart
Springer	Kaz Garas
Carla Cord	Linda Gray
Bonnie Buehler	Kimberly Beck
Bo Buehler	Royal Dano
Jay Kamens	Norman Burton
Kaiserman	Charles Siebert
David Roerick	Edward Bell

Peyton Place: The Next Generation
(NBC, May 13, 1985)
Twentieth Century Fox Television
Executive Producer: Michael Filerman
Co-Producer: Terry Morse Jr.
Written by: Rita Lakin
Directed by: Larry Elikann

Twenty years after Allison MacKenzie's disappearance, her daughter Megan returns to Peyton Place. This creates resentment and conflict with Kelly Carson, Allison's younger sister. When it appears that Allison may have been a victim of suicide, attorney Steven Cord investigates and discovers otherwise.

Cast

Constance Carson	Dorothy Malone
Dr. Michael Rossi	Ed Nelson
Betty Harrington Cord	Barbara Parkins
Elliot Carson	Tim O'Connor
Norman Harrington	Christopher Connelly
Steven Cord	James Douglas
Rita Harrington	Patricia Morrow
Ada Jacks	Evelyn Scott
Hannah Cord	Ruth Warrick
Dana Harrington	Bruce Greenwood
Megan MacKenzie	Marguerite Hickey
Kelly Carson	Deborah Goodrich
Dorian Blake	John Beck
Joey Harrington	Tony Quinn

Biographies

Lola Albright *(Constance MacKenzie—temporary replacement)*

Lola Albright began her movie career in the late 1940s and drew attention for her role in the 1949 boxing film *Champion* starring Kirk Douglas. In 1958, she was cast as Edie Hart, the sultry nightclub singer, in Blake Edward's *Peter Gunn* (1958–1961) which starred Craig Stevens and co-starred Herschel Bernardi. In 1959, Albright was nominated for an Emmy Award for Best Supporting Actress in a Dramatic Series. She recorded two albums, *Lola Wants You* and *Dreamsville*, the latter accompanied by Henry Mancini and his orchestra. In late 1965, she replaced Dorothy Malone (for about six weeks) in the role of Constance MacKenzie on *Peyton Place*.

Her major film credits include: *Where Were You When the Lights Went Out?*, *The Impossible Years*, *Lord Love a Duck*, *The Way West*, *Kid Galahad*, *A Cold Wind in August*, and *The Good Humor Man*.

Her many network television appearances include: *Airwolf*, *Quincy M.E.*, *The Incredible Hulk*, *Switch*, *Terraces*, *Columbo*, *Starsky and Hutch*, *McMillan and Wife*, *Police Story*, *Medical Center*, *Kojak*, *The Man from UNCLE*, *Bonanza*, *How I Spent My Summer Vacation*, *Branded*, *Laredo*, *Rawhide*, *Burke's Law*, *Wagon Train*, *Alfred Hitchcock Presents*, *Adventures in Paradise* and *General Electric Theater*.

Mary Anderson *(Catherine Harrington)*

Mary Anderson made her screen debut in *Gone with the Wind*. She appeared in numerous films until the early 1950s then occasionally acted in television until the mid 1960s.

A partial list of her film work includes: *The Song of Bernadette, Lifeboat, Wilson, To Each His Own, Whispering City, The Underworld Story,* and *I, the Jury*.

Her television shows include: *Daniel Boone, The Travels of Jamie McPheeters, Lawman, The Californians, Perry Mason, Studio One, Mike Hammer, Tombstone Territory, Climax* and *Lux Video Theatre*.

Warner Anderson *(Matt Swain)*

Warner Anderson began his career as a child actor in silent films. He later appeared on Broadway prior to his re-entry into films in the 1940s. In the 1950s, he starred on TV as Detective Lt. Ben Guthrie opposite Tom Tully in *The Lineup* (1954–1959). He left the cast of *Peyton Place* after the first year but remained as the narrator for the entire series run.

His film credits include: *The Lineup* (the feature film version), *A Lawless Street, Blackboard Jungle, The Violent Men, Drum Beat, The Caine Mutiny, The Yellow Tomahawk, City Story, The Star, The Guest, Detective Story, Go for Broke, Only the Valiant, Santa Fe, Destination Moon, Command Decision, Song of the Thin Man, Dark Delusion, The Beginning of the End, Three Wise Fools, Objective, Burma!,* and *Destination Tokyo*.

His TV appearance include: *The Rockford Files, Ironside, O'Hara, U.S. Treasury, Bearcats, The Interns, The Immortal, Death Valley Days, Pursuit* and *Climax*.

Kimberly Beck *(Kim Schuster)*

Kimberly Beck was born in Glendale, California and made her screen debut at age two in the film *Torpedo Run* which starred Glenn Ford. At age ten, she appeared on *Peyton Place* in the pivotal role of Kim Schuster. She continued to act in films and television well into adulthood.

Her many TV credits include: *The Commish, FBI: The Untold Stories, Sons and Daughters, The Law and Harry McGraw, LA Law, Dynasty, Mike Hammer, Crazy Like a Fox, Hunter, T.J. Hooker, Webster, Capitol* (as *Julie Clegg*), *Matt Houston, Buck Rogers in the 25th Century, B.J. and the Bear, Fantasy Island, The Hardy Boys/Nancy Drew Mysteries, Murder in Peyton Place, Eight is Enough, Rich Man, Poor Man, Book II, General Hospital, Bonanza, My Three Sons, Land of the Giants,* and *The Virginian*.

Her film appearances include: *Independence Day, False Identity, Messenger of Death, Maid to Order, Yours, Mine and Ours, Marnie* and *The FBI Story*.

Joan Blackman *(Marion Fowler)*

Californian Joan Blackman first appeared on television in the 1959 syndicated series *Hawkeye* and *The Last of the Mohicans* which starred John Hart and Lon Chaney Jr. She then appeared in seven feature films before guesting on numerous network TV series throughout the 1960s. She was seen infrequently in the 1970s. In 1990 she appeared in the English TV series entitled *The Castle of Adventure*.

Her film credits include: *Return to Waterloo, One Man Shivers, Moonrunners, Macon County Line, Pets, Daring Game, The Destructors, Intimacy, Twilight of Honor, Kid Galahad, Blue Hawaii, The Great Imposter, Visit to a Small Planet, Career,* and *Good Day for a Hanging*.

Her television work includes: *Doc Elliot, Ghost Story, Run for Your Life, Gunsmoke, I Spy, Kraft Suspense Theatre, Bonanza, Perry Mason, Slattery's People, The Dick Powell Show,* and *Goodyear Theatre*.

Henry Beckman *(George Anderson)*

Henry Beckman was born in Halifax, Nova Scotia. Prior to his stint on *Peyton Place*, Beckman played Commander Paul Richards in the *Flash Gordon* TV series in the early 1950s, and appeared as Mulligan in *I'm Dickens, He's Fenster* (1962–1963). In the late 1960s, Beckman portrayed Captain Roland Francis Clancey in *Here Come the Brides* (1968–1969) and in the mid 70s appeared as Harris Mark in *Bronk* (1974–1975).

A partial list of his several hundred television credits include: *The Chris Isaak Show, Honey, I Shrunk the Kids, The X Files, The Marshal, The Outer Limits, Street Legal, The Beachcombers, MacGyver, War and Remembrance, St. Elsewhere, Simon and Simon, Fame, Trapper John M.D., Quincy M.E., Welcome Back Kotter, The Six Million Dollar Man, Barney Miller, Police Story, Ironside, Cannon, Gunsmoke, Shaft, Columbo, Night Gallery, Wild Wild West, Run for Your Life, Perry Mason, McHale's Navy, Combat, Dr. Kildare, Route 66, Laramie, Peter Gunn,* and *Hazel*.

His film work includes: *Death Hunt, Silver Streak, Sweet Charity, Madigan, The Satin Bug, Kiss Me Stupid, Dead Ringer* and *13 West Street*.

Patricia Breslin *(Laura Brooks)*

Born and raised in New York, Patricia Breslin first came to prominence as Mandy Peoples in the NBC TV series *People's Choice* (1955–1958) co-starring Jackie Cooper. After *Peyton Place*, Breslin appeared as Meg Bentley R.N. on *General Hospital*.

Her television work includes: *The Virginian, The Alfred Hitchcock Hour, The Greatest Show on Earth, Dr. Kildare, The Dick Powell Show, The Twilight Zone, Bonanza, Thriller, Adventures in Paradise, The Donna Reed Show, Tales of Wells Fargo, The New Breed, The Rebel, The Rifleman, The Detectives, Outlaws, Tate, Hotel de Paree, The Millionaire, Maverick, Alcoa Theatre, Schlitz Playhouse of Stars, Robert Montgomery Presents, The Web, Kraft Television Theatre, Studio One, Hallmark Hall of Fame,* and *Suspense*.

In the 1960s, Breslin also appeared in two William Castle thrillers: *I Saw What You Did* and *Homocidal*.

David Canary *(Russ Gehring)*

David Canary was born in Elwood, Indiana and later raised in Ohio. He graduated from the University of Cincinnati with a degree in music and made his Broadway debut in *Great Day in the Morning* (starring Colleen Dewhurst).

He first appeared on television in *Peyton Place* and made his film debut in *Hombre* (which starred Paul Newman). Soon after, Canary was cast as Candy Canaday on *Bonanza* (1967–1970, 1972–1973). From 1984 to 2010, Canary portrayed Adam Chandler (and twin brother Stuart) on *All My Children* (winning five Best Actor Daytime Emmy Awards).

Additional TV guest appearances include: *Touched by an Angel, Law and Order, Remember WENN, King of America, Another World, Search for Tomorrow, The Dain Curse, S.W.A.T., The Rookies, Melvin Purvis G-Man, Kung Fu, Police Story, Incident on a Dark Street, Alias Smith and Jones, Bearcats, Hawaii Five-O, The F.B.I., Cimarron Strip, Dundee and the Culhane,* and *Gunsmoke*.

His film credits include: *Johnny Firecloud, Posse, Shark's Treasure,* and *The St. Valentine's Day Massacre*.

Everett Chambers *(Producer)*

Everett Chambers began his television producing career on the series *Johnny Staccato* (1959–1960) which starred John Cassavetes. Over a span of 35 years, he produced such series as *Airwolf, Partners in Crime, Columbo* (which earned him 5 Emmy nominations), and *Peyton Place*.

His list of network television movies as a supervising producer/producer include: *Incident in a Small Town, Beverly Hills Madam, A Matter of Sex* (executive producer), *Will There Really Be a Morning?, Berlin Tunnel 21, Turnover Smith, B.A.D. Cats,*

Nero Wolfe, Street Killing (executive producer), *Twin Detectives, They Only Come Out at Night* (executive producer), *Can Ellen Be Saved?, The Girl Most Likely To, The Great American Beauty Contest, Trouble Comes to Town,* and *Night Slaves.*

Michael Christian *(Joe Rossi)*

Michael Christian first trained at the Actors Studio then later studied at the Desilu Professional Playhouse in California. He won the role of Joe Rossi once Paul Monash saw him in a guest role on ABC's *The Felony Squad.* After a year on *Peyton Place,* Christian pursued a film career. In the early 1970s, he starred opposite Troy Donahue in *The Legend of Frank Woods,* then co-starred in the western *El Savage* (The Savage) with another *Peyton Place* alumnus, Stephen Oliver. Christian was then cast opposite Shelly Winters and Slim Pickens in *Poor Pretty Eddie.* His stellar portrayal of a psychopath enabled him to write, produce and star in *Midnight Rider* (co-starring Keenan Wynn). Christian later wrote a script for the original *Terminators.* In the 1990s, he produced and starred in *Private Obsession* (with Bo Svenson and Shannon Whirry) then starred with Chris Mitchum in *Body Count.* He later played the lead role in the sci-fi thriller *Wasteland Justice* (which featured Vernon Wells of *Road Warrior* fame).

Christopher Connelly *(Norman Harrington)*

Christopher Connelly was born in Wichita, Kansas. He began his television career in the early 1960s appearing in shows such as *The Alfred Hitchcock Hour, The Lieutenant, The Fugitive* and *Voyage to the Bottom of the Sea.* After *Peyton Place* ended its run, Connelly guest starred on numerous network TV series. In 1974, he was cast as Moses Pray in the short lived series *Paper Moon* which co-starred Jodie Foster. (Ironically, Ryan O'Neal, Connelly's brother on *Peyton Place,* played the same role in the feature film version.)

His film credits include: *Strike Commando, The Messenger, Cobra Mission, Foxtrap, Liar's Moon, Manhattan Baby, Benji, Earthbound,* and *They Only Kill Their Masters.*

His many TV appearances include: *Peyton Place: The Next Generation, Airwolf, Matt Houston, Fantasy Island, Simon & Simon, CHiPs, Eight is Enough, The Martian Chronicles, Trapper John M.D., The Love Boat, Salvage 1, Police Story, Murder in Peyton Place, Quincy M.E., Kit Carson and the Mountain Men, Petrocelli, Medical Story, Ironside, Cannon, Marcus Welby, Barnaby Jones, Owen Marshall, Counselor at Law, Mannix, Night Gallery, Love, American Style, Dan August, Mission: Impossible, Bonanza, Daniel Boone,* and *The Mod Squad.*

Ruby Dee *(Alma Miles)*

Although born in Cleveland, Ohio, Ruby Dee considers herself a product of Harlem, where she grew up and began her career as a member of the American Negro Theatre. She received her B.A. from Hunter College, and later studied acting with Paul Mann, Lloyd Richards and Morris Carnovsky.

Her most recent roles have been in *American Gangster,* with Denzel Washington and Russell Crowe; in *Steam,* with Ally Sheedy; and in the independent film *All About Us.* In 2005, she starred in *Naming Number 2,* a New Zealand comedy-drama which won the Audience Award at the 2006 Sundance Film Festival and for which she was awarded New Zealand's highest acting honors. Ms. Dee is featured with Julie Harris in *The Way Back Home.* She was also featured in the Oprah Winfrey television production of *Their Eyes Were Watching God.*

Some of her favorite roles on stage and screen include: Lutiebelle in *Purlie Victorious* (written by her late husband, Ossie Davis); Ruth in *A Raisin in the Sun;* Lena in *Boesman and Lena,* for which she received an Obie and a Drama Desk award; and Mary Tyrone in *A Long Day's Journey Into Night,* for which she received a Cable ACE award. Other notable credits include: *Anna Lucasta, Wedding Band, St. Lucy's Eyes, The Jackie Robinson*

Story, Uptight (which she co-wrote), *Buck and the Preacher, Countdown at Kusini* (which she co-produced with Delta Sigma Theta sorority), *Do The Right Thing, Jungle Fever, Peyton Place, Go Tell It on the Mountain, The Stand,* and *Having Our Say.* She has received several Emmy nominations, and in 1991, won an Emmy for her performance in *Decoration Day.*

In 2006, Ms. Dee released the selected speeches and writings of Ossie Davis in *Life Lit by Some Large Vision,* in bookstores now. She is also the author of two children's books, *Tower to Heaven* and *Two Ways to Count to Ten;* a book of poetry and short stories, *My One Good Nerve* (which she has adapted into a solo performance piece); and *With Ossie and Ruby: In This Life Together,* a joint autobiography co-authored with her late husband—the audio version received a Grammy Award in the Spoken Word category. She has also narrated several audio books, including Zora Neale Hurston's *Their Eyes Were Watching God* (for which performance she won an Audie Award).

In 1988, Ms. Dee was inducted into the Theatre Hall of Fame. With Mr. Davis, she has been inducted into the NAACP Image Award Hall of Fame, awarded the Silver Circle Award by the Academy of Television Arts and Science, the National Medal of Arts Award, and the Screen Actors Guild's Lifetime Achievement Award. In December 2004, Ms. Dee and Mr. Davis were recipients of the John F. Kennedy Center Honors.

Tom Del Ruth *(Cinematographer)*

Tom Del Ruth began his career as an assistant cameraman on such films as *Doctor Dolittle, Divorce American Style, Valley of the Dolls, Planet of the Apes* and *Butch Cassidy and the Sundance Kid.* He later worked as a camera operator on *The Front Page, The Day of the Locust, Smile, Gable and Lombard, The Duchess and the Dirtwater Fox, The Outlaw Josie Wales,* and *The Shootist.*

As a cinematographer his filmology includes: *Flipped* (the new Rob Reiner film), *Leave It to Beaver, Amore, Little Sister, Look Who's Talking Too, Look Who's Talking, The Running Man, Cross*

My Heart, Quicksilver, Stand By Me, The Breakfast Club, Fandango, Impulse, Get Crazy, and *Death Wish II.*

His extensive television work (as a Director of Photography) includes: *Studio 60 on the Sunset Strip, The Book of Daniel, Code Breakers, Heartless, The West Wing, Charmed, It Came from the Sky, Down Will Come Baby, Chasing the Dragon, JAG, Abandoned and Deceived, ER, Next Door, Royce, Shattered Image, House of Secrets, The X Files, Wolf, Dream Breakers, Spies, Who is Julia, Blind Justice, Intimate Agony, Best Kept Secrets, Who Will Love My Children, Million Dollar Infield, Elvis and the Beauty Queen,* and *The Last Convertible.*

Richard De Roy *(Executive Script Consultant)*

Richard De Roy was the initial head writer on *Peyton Place* and remained with the series for most of its run. In addition to his work as a freelance writer in episodic television, De Roy also served as a script consultant/story editor on series such as *Father Dowling Mysteries, Remington Steele, Hart to Hart,* and *Sons and Daughters.*

His TV writing credits include: *Generations, Intimate Agony, The Other Victim, The Dream Merchants, Hawaii Five-O, Harold Robbins' 79 Park Avenue, Murder in Peyton Place, A Howling in the Woods, The Name of the Game, The Partridge Family, Room 222, The Survivors, The Flying Nun, The Rat Patrol, The Girl from U.N.C.L.E., The Rogues, The Twilight Zone, Mr. Novak, 77 Sunset Strip, Checkmate, Surfside 6, Kraft Television Theatre,* and *Studio One.*

Walter Doniger *(Director)*

Walter Doniger began his career as a screenwriter in the 1940s and 1950s on such films as *Rope of Sand* (which earned him a Golden Globe Nomination for Best Screenplay), *Tokyo Joe,* and *Along the Great Divide.* He then began to direct some of his own screenplays such as *The Steel Jungle, The Steel Cage,* and *Duffy of San Quentin*. He also wrote for television series such as *Perry Mason, The Dick Powell Show, Tombstone Territory,* and *Cheyenne* then began directing as well.

Doniger was known for his creative camera work that enhanced his storytelling.

His many directorial efforts include: *Kentucky Woman, Shannon, Mad Bull, Marcus Welby M.D., Switch, McCloud, Lucas Tanner, Barnaby Jones, Kung Fu, Ghost Story, Owen Marshall: Counselor at Law, Sarge, Night Gallery, The Virginian, Bracken's World, Judd for the Defense, The Man Who Never Was, Mr. Novak, The Travels of Jamie McPheeters, Michael Shayne, Outlaws, Hong Kong, Lockup, Men into Space, Bat Masterson, Highway Patrol* and *Maverick*.

James Douglas *(Steven Cord)*

James Douglas first appeared in the 1957 film *Fear Strikes Out* (the baseball story of Jimmy Persall). He began to work in television shortly after and in 1965 joined the cast of *Peyton Place*. He later appeared as Grant Coleman on *As the World Turns*, and as Dr. Marcus Polk on *One Life to Live*.

His additional television credits include: *Spenser for Hire, Peyton Place: The Next Generation, The Bold Ones, Ironside, A Clear and Present Danger, 12 O'Clock High, The Detectives Starring Robert Taylor, Death Valley Days, Adventures in Paradise, M Squad, Dragnet, The Life and Legend of Wyatt Earp,* and *The Millionaire*.

Film appearances include: *Sweet Bird of Youth, A Thunder of Drums, G.I. Blues, Time Limit, Until They Sail, The Helen Morgan Story, Beginning of the End,* and *Designing Woman*.

Dan Duryea *(Eddie Jacks)*

Dan Duryea was an accomplished actor on the Broadway stage before his entry into films in the 1940s. He earned acclaim in *Dead End*, followed by *The Little Foxes*, then appeared in the film version (which starred Bette Davis). He portrayed numerous villains with an off-beat demeanor in a variety of films and as a result achieved a cult status. In the 1950s, he began to work in television, and starred in *The New Adventures of China Smith* (1953–1954). He continued to work in movies and television until the late 1960s.

Some of his many films include: *Incident at Phantom Hill, The Flight of the Phoenix, Slaughter on Tenth Avenue, Night Passage, The Burglar, Battle Hymn, Storm Fear, The Marauders, This is My Love, Silver Lode, World for Ransom, Thunder Bay, Chicago Calling, Winchester 73, Criss Cross, Another Part of the Forest, Black Bart, Along Came Jones, None but the Lonely Heart, Ministry of Fear, Sahara, Pride of the Yankees,* and *The Little Foxes.*

His television work includes: *Combat, The Monroes, The Virginian, The Loner, The Long Hot Summer, Daniel Boone, Bonanza, Burke's Law, Wagon Train, The Alfred Hitchcock Hour, Route 66, Rawhide, The Eleventh Hour, The Wide Country, Naked City, Tales of Wells Fargo, Laramie, Checkmate, Riverboat, Adventures in Paradise, The Twilight Zone, The David Niven Show,* and *Climax.*

John Erman *(Director)*

John Erman came into prominence in the world of television with the film *Green Eyes*, which starred Paul Winfield. This earned him the Humanitas Prize and opportunity to direct *Roots* which earned him a Director's Guild Award and Emmy Nomination for Best Director. He later won an Emmy for *Who Will Love My Children* starring Ann-Margaret. Erman would team again with her in several acclaimed TV films including: *A Streetcar Named Desire, The Two Mrs. Greenvilles, Our Sons* (Erman's second film about AIDS), *Queen,* and *Scarlett* (an eight hour mini-series for CBS).

Erman's other notable achievements include: *An Early Frost* (which earned him a second Director's Guild Award and fourth Emmy nomination), and *The Attic: The Hiding of Anne Frank* (which like *An Early Frost* received an Emmy nomination for Best Picture and earned Erman the Peabody Award plus his second Christopher Award).

Additional TV productions include: *David, Stella, The Last Best Year,* the adaptation of Anne Tyler's Pulitzer Prize-winning novel *Breathing Lessons* (for Hallmark), *The Boys Next Door* (also for Hallmark), and *Ellen Foster.* His mini-series for CBS include: *Only Love, The Doris Duke Story,* and *Victoria and Albert.*

Erman has taught at the Columbia Graduate Film School, and at Fordham University.

Richard Evans *(Paul Hanley)*

Richard Evans appeared in over 300 film and television productions including: *Islands in the Stream, The Nickel Ride,* and *Dirty Little Billy.* He played the continuing role of Paul Hanley in *Peyton Place* during the first season. Evans wrote, produced, and photographed one of the first anti-war films of the 1960s, *Toys on a Field of Blue.* In 1971, Evans completed the feature film *Original: Do Not Project,* the story of a young filmmaker that was shown at the Cannes Festival in 1972. In recent years, he has worked as a producer/director in the theatre staging plays by Sam Sheppard and David Mamet. In 2007, he directed the film *Shadow of Rain.*

His television work (as an actor) includes: *Deadly Care, The A-Team, Hart to Hart, Lou Grant, Quincy M.E., Barnaby Jones, How the West Was Won, Mannix, Cannon, Cry Rape, The F.B.I., Bonanza, Lassie, Lancer, The Virginian, The Mod Squad, The Guns of Will Sonnett, The High Chaparral, Star Trek, The Big Valley, Gunsmoke, The Iron Horse, Felony Squad, Perry Mason, The Fugitive, Dr. Kildare, The Lieutenant, Channing, Mr. Novak, Redigo, Temple Houston, Empire, Stoney Burke, The Eleventh Hour, Lawman, The Rifleman, Checkmate, Cheyenne, Sea Hunt, Laramie, Hennesey, The Rebel, Bronco,* and *Wagon Train.*

Mia Farrow *(Allison MacKenzie)*

Mia Farrow was born into a show business family as the daughter of actress Maureen O'Sullivan and director John Farrow. After her portrayal of Allison MacKenzie for two seasons on *Peyton Place*, she went on to star and co-star in more than forty feature films. She has won numerous acting awards and is well known for her humanitarian work as a UNICEF Goodwill Ambassador. In recent years she has been very involved in humanitarian activities in Darfur, Chad, and the Central African Republic.

    Her filmography includes: *Be Kind Rewind, Purpose, Coming Soon, Angela Mooney, Reckless, Miami Rhapsody, Widows' Peak, Husbands and Wives, Shadows and Fog, Alice, Crimes and Misdemeanors, New York Stories, Another Woman, September, Radio Days, Hannah and Her Sisters, The Purple Rose of Cairo, Supergirl, Broadway Danny Rose, Zelig, A Midsummer Night's Sex Comedy, Hurricane, Death on the Nile, Avalanche, A Wedding, Full Circle, The Great Gatsby, Docteur Popaul, Follow Me!, Blind Terror, John and Mary, Secret Ceremony, Rosemary's Baby, A Dandy in Aspic,* and *Guns at Batasi.*

Frank Ferguson *(Eli Carson)*

Frank Ferguson began his theatrical career as an actor/director with the Pasadena Playhouse. He entered films in the 1940s and in the mid 1950s began to appear frequently on television as well. Ferguson portrayed ranch hand, Gus Broeberg, in *My Friend Flicka* (1955–56) and ten years later was seen as Eli Carson on *Peyton Place* (1965–1969). Ferguson reprised the role of Eli in the NBC daytime drama *Return to Peyton Place* (1972–1974). He continued to appear on television until the late 1970s.

    A partial list of his many film credits include: *The Great Sioux Massacre, Those Calloways, Hush, Hush Sweet Charlotte, Pocketful of Miracles, Sunrise at Campobello, Andy Hardy Comes Home, Man of the West, The Light in the Forest, Trial, The McConnell Story,*

Battle Cry, The Violent Men, Young at Heart, A Star is Born, House of Wax, Trouble Along the Way, The Blue Gardenia, and *Santa Fe.*

His several hundred TV appearances include: *How the West Was Won, Little House on the Prairie, The Waltons, McMillan and Wife, Kung Fu, Alias Smith and Jones, Cannon, Adam-12, Green Acres, Land of the Giants, The Andy Griffith Show, Perry Mason, Wagon Train, The Twilight Zone, The Third Man, The Virginian, Leave It to Beaver, McHale's Navy, Cheyenne, Surfside 6, Tales of Wells Fargo, Maverick, Have Gun–Will Travel, Riverboat,* and *Wanted: Dead or Alive.*

John Findlater *(Jeff Kramer)*

John Findlater first appeared in the film *Where Angels Go Trouble Follows!* which starred Rosalind Russell. After *Peyton Place* ended, Findlater appeared sporadically in films and television throughout the 1970s and 1980s.

His movie credits include: *Vengeance of a Soldier, Meteor, Airport,* and *With Six You Get Eggroll.*

His television appearances include: *Rags to Riches, Highway to Heaven, Simon & Simon, Dynasty, Quincy M.E., Nero Wolfe, Project U.F.O., Kingston: Confidential, Switch, Barnaby Jones, Room 222, Bracken's World,* and *Marcus Welby M.D.*

Michael Gleason *(Staff Writer 1965–1968)*

Michael Gleason began his career writing for western series such as *Maverick, Laramie,* and *Rawhide.* He later wrote for *It's a Man's World, Mr. Novak,* and *My Favorite Martian.* After *Peyton Place,* Gleason co-created and wrote for *The Survivors* and *Paris 7000.* He later became a writer/producer on *McCloud, The Six Million Dollar Man,* and *The Oregon Trail* (which he also co-created); and wrote and executive produced *Rich Man, Poor Man, Book II.*

In the early 1980s, Gleason created the NBC series

Remington Steele and served as writer/executive producer for four seasons.

In recent years his writing credits include TV movies for the Hallmark and Lifetime Channels: *Murder 101, Silent Partner, Wild Card, Acting Up,* and *Thick as Thieves.* His episodic TV work includes: *Charmed, Martial Law, Police Academy, The Burning Zone, Lois and Clark, Nash Bridges,* and *Diagnosis Murder.*

Bruce Gordon *(Gus Chernak)*

Bruce Gordon first appeared on Broadway from the early to the mid 1940s as Officer Klein in *Arsenic and Old Lace.* He made his film debut in the 1949 Marx Brothers film *Love Happy.* Throughout the 1950s, he acted in numerous TV shows, and during the 1958–1959 season, Gordon hosted and starred in nine episodes of NBC's *Behind Closed Doors.* Audiences best remember him for his sinister portrayal of mobster Frank Nitti in *The Untouchables* (1959–1963). In 1966, Gordon co-starred in the CBS series *Run, Buddy Run* opposite musician Jack Sheldon. He retired from acting in 1989.

His film appearances include: *Ishtar, Timerider, Piranha, Hello Down There, Tower of London,* and *The Buccaneer.*

His lengthy list of TV credits include: *Simon & Simon, The Fall Guy, Joe Forrester, Banacek, Here' Lucy, Ironside, Bonanza, Gentle Ben, Mannix, Get Smart, Tarzan, The Flying Nun, The Girl from U.N.C.L.E., The Defenders, Naked City, Car 54, Where Are You?, Adventures in Paradise, Sugarfoot, Peter Gunn, Maverick, Gunsmoke, Tightrope, One Step Beyond, The Californians, Whirlybirds, Decoy,* and *M-Squad.*

Lee Grant *(Stella Chernak)*

While still in her teens, Lee Grant established herself as a formidable Broadway talent, winning the Critics Circle Award for her performance as the shoplifter in *Detective Story.* She recreated this portrayal on film, garnering the Cannes Film Festival award as Best Actress, her first Academy Award nomination and an invitation into the prestigious Actors Studio. Grant's impressive film debut was cut short by the McCarthy Era entertainment industry blacklist. After twelve years, she resumed a stunning film career, beginning with a 1966 Emmy Award for *Peyton Place* and culminating with a 1976 Academy Award for *Shampoo*. During this time, she also received much attention for her riveting performance in the 1967 Academy Award winning picture *In the Heat of the Night*, another Emmy Award for *The Neon Ceiling* and Academy Award nominations for *The Landlord* and *Voyage of the Damned*.

Since 1980, Grant has concentrated on her directorial efforts. She and her husband, Joseph Feury, launched an independent production company in 1982 and have since produced a number of award winning films. Their credits include five documentaries, made for HBO's *America Undercover* series. *When Women Kill* profiled women serving prison sentences for homicide convictions. *What Sex Am I?* explored transvestite and transsexual lifestyles. *Battered* looked at the issue of domestic violence. *Women on Trial* examined court custody battles. *Down and Out in America* examined homelessness throughout the country and garnered both an Academy Award and a Cable Ace Award in 1986. Of the company's made-for-television movies, Grant received the 1987 Directors Guild Award for the CBS film *Nobody's Child* and the 1989 FIPA D'Argent at the Cannes International Television Festival for *No Place Like Home*, also on CBS. In the early 1990s she directed three more television movies—*Seasons of the Heart* for CBS, *Reunion* for CBS and *Following Her Heart* for NBC. Grant also returned to the screen as an actress, working on network television and in the feature films *Defending Your Life* and *It's My Party*.

She has directed several *Intimate Portraits* for Lifetime Television, among them *Vanessa Redgrave, Lauren Bacall, Mia Farrow, Tipper Gore, Elizabeth Taylor* and *Gloria Steinem*–Lifetime's 100th portrait. Ms. Grant received a Gilda Award for her

Intimate Portrait of Madeline Kahn, and *Intimate Portrait Bella Abzug* was the recipient of a Gracie Award. Ms. Grant directed the documentary, *Confronting the Crisis: Childcare in America,* which aired on Lifetime in April 1999. She recently directed *The Loretta Claiborne Story* for Disney/ABC, *The Gun Deadlock* for Lifetime Television and a *PBS American Masters on Sidney Poitier.* In 2006 she directed an HBO documentary on Kirk and Michael Douglas, *A Father, A Son–Once Upon a Time in Hollywood.* Grant, with husband Joe Feury, produced a critically acclaimed documentary on medics and the wounded in Iraq, *Baghdad ER,* which was released in 2006 on HBO and won the Emmy and the Peabody Award. Her most recent project is directing an *American Masters on Robert Altman* for PBS.

Mariette Hartley *(Dr. Claire Morton)*

Emmy Award-winning actress Mariette Hartley first appeared in the western *Ride the High Country* (1962) which starred Joel McCrea and Randolph Scott; followed by a role in Hitchcock's *Marnie.* She went on to guest star in many network television shows, and made a series of popular TV commercials with James Garner. She also co-hosted the ABC morning show *AM America.* In 2006, she performed her one woman show *If You Get to Bethlehem, You've Gone Too Far,* based on her best-selling biography *Breaking the Silence.*

Her many TV credits include: *Law and Order: Special Victims Unit, Cold Case, Grey's Anatomy, Saving Grace, NCIS, Caroline in the City, Perry Mason: The Case of the Telltale Talk Show Host, Murder She Wrote, Diagnosis Murder, WIOU* (as Liz McVay), *Goodnight, Beantown, The Love Boat, M.A.D.D. – Mothers Against Drunk Drivers (The Candy Lightner Story), The Rockford Files, M*A*S*H, Little House on the Prairie, Columbo, Police Woman, McCloud, Barnaby Jones, Gunsmoke, Emergency,* and *The Bob Newhart Show.*

Jeffrey Hayden *(Director)*

Jeffrey Hayden has directed more than 400 television shows for the major networks, including: *In the Heat of the Night, Magnum, Cagney & Lacey, Quincy, Ironside, Mannix, Palmerstown, The Bold Ones, Peyton Place, Route 66, 77 Sunset Strip, The Andy Griffith Show, The Donna Reed Show,* and *Leave It to Beaver,* among others.

After graduating from the University of North Carolina, Chapel Hill, he went to New York where he directed many live shows in the Golden Age of Television: *Omnibus, NBC Color Specials,* and *The Philco-Goodyear Playhouse,* where he directed Paul Newman, Inger Stevens, Walter Matthau, EG Marshall, and James Dean, in powerful dramatic roles. This led to an invitation to join MGM in Hollywood where he directed his first feature film, *The Vintage.*

Along with his film and television work, Mr. Hayden continued producing and directing in the theatre; *Summer & Smoke, Desire Under the Elms, The Fatal Weakness, Candida, Dark at the Top of the Stairs, Awake and Sing, The Country Girl, Duet for One, The Front Page, Death of a Salesman, The Sunshine Boys,* in New York, at Washington's Kennedy Center, in Los Angeles, and regional theaters around the country.

More recently, he wrote, produced, and directed two award-winning documentaries for PBS: *Primary Colors, The Story of Corita,* and *Children in America's Schools with Bill Moyers.* They earned him an Emmy, Cine Golden Eagle, AFI Award, The Edward R Murrow Award, and the NEA's Golden Medal. Other awards for his television work include the California Governor's Media Award, The Robert E. Sherwood Award, and the NAACP Image Award. Married to Eva Marie Saint, they have collaborated on many theatrical productions and continue to do so in *Love Letters* and *On the Divide: The Works of Willa Cather,* with Mr. Hayden co-starring as well as directing.

Gary Haynes *(Chris Webber)*

Gary Haynes grew up in Southern California and first appeared on television in an episode of *Ben Casey*. In the spring of 1966, during the second season of *Peyton Place*, he was cast as the visually handicapped younger brother of Lee Webber. Haynes also appeared in *The Time Tunnel* as well as the television movie: *The President's Plane is Missing*.

Robert Hogan *(Tom Winter)*

Robert Hogan was last seen on the New York stage in the Play Company's production of *Rainbow Kiss*. On Broadway, he created the role of Matthew Markinson in Aaron Sorkin's *A Few Good Men*. Also on Broadway: the Ghost of Hamlet's Father, and First Player, in the Roundabout Theatre Company's production of *Hamlet*. Other New York stage performances: *Accomplices* (The New Group), *Boy* (Primary Stages), *What Didn't Happen* and *On the Bum* (Playwrights Horizons), *Further Than the Furthest Thing* (Manhattan Theatre Club), *Baby Dance* (Lucille Lortel Theater), *Hope is the Thing With Feathers* (Drama Dept.), *Waiting for Lefty* (directed by Joanne Woodward), *Major Crimes* and *Lighting Up the Two-Year-Old* (Actors Studio Theatre), *Rutherford and Son* (Mint Theater), *In the Western Garden* (EST) and *Never the Sinner*, for which he won an Outer Critics Circle Award for his portrayal of famed attorney, Clarence Darrow. Regional highlights: the world premiere of William Kennedy's play, *Grand View* at Capitol Repertory in Albany, and a Helen Hayes Award nomination for the role of Hogan in Eugene O'Neill's *Moon for the Misbegotten* at the Arena Stage in Washington, DC.

Hogan's many film roles include portraying JFK in *Prince Jack* and performances in *Day Zero*, *Welcome to Academia* (in post-production), *Species II*, *Lady in Red*, *Sweetland*, *Maze* (director: Rob Morrow), *Town Diary*, *Blue Xmas*, *Gone Are the Dayes*, *Greenwich Village Story*, *In Memory of Us*, *Hamburger: The Motion Picture*, and the classic Michael Crighton film, *Westworld*.

He also appeared in over 150 primetime shows including: *Law & Order* (Judge Hugo Bright), *Law & Order: Criminal Intent*, HBO's *The Wire*, *Third Watch*, *Cosby*, *Deadline*, *Hill Street Blues* and *M*A*S*H*.

On a personal note, Hogan is a graduate of the American Academy of Dramatic Arts and studied under Stella Adler. He lives in New York City with his wife, Mary, the author of seven popular young adult novels.

Wilfred Hyde-White *(Martin Peyton—temporary replacement)*

Wilfred Hyde-White was a renowned English character actor whose career spanned five decades. He worked consistently on stage before becoming a fixture in British films of the late 1940s and the 1950s. He also appeared on Broadway and was nominated for two Tony Awards as best actor. He appeared as a regular cast member in the US TV series *Buck Rogers in the 25th Century*, *Battlestar Gallactica*, and *The Associates*.

His notable British films include: *Elephant Boy*, *The Winslow Boy*, *The Passionate Friends*, *Adam and Evelyne*, *The Third Man*, *Last Holiday*, *The Story of Gilbert and Sullivan*, *The Million Pound Note*, *Betrayed*, *Quentin Durward*, *The Magic Christian*, *The Vicious Circle*, *North West Frontier*, and *Libel*.

His American filmography includes: *The Toy*, *Xanadu*, *Oh, God! Book II*, *Gaily Gaily*, *The Million Eyes of Sumuru*, *John Goldfarb, Please Come Home!*, *My Fair Lady*, *On the Double*, and *Let's Make Love*.

His television work includes: *Fanny Hill*, *Filthy Rich*, *Father Murphy*, *Fantasy Island*, *Laverne and Shirley*, *Vega$*, *Colombo*, *Cool Million*, *The Most Deadly Game*, *It Takes a Thief*, *Fear No Evil*, *The Name of the Game*, *Daniel Boone*, *Mission: Impossible*, and *The Twilight Zone*.

Diana Hyland *(Susan Winter)*

Originally from Ohio, Diana Hyland made her Broadway debut as Heavenly Finley in *Sweet Bird of Youth*. On daytime TV, she appeared on NBC's *Young Doctor Malone* (1958–1963). Throughout the 1960s and well into the 1970s, she guested on such shows as *The Defenders, Naked City, Ben Casey, The Twilight Zone, Kraft Suspense Theatre, The Wackiest Ship in the Army, A Man Called Shenandoah, The Man from U.N.C.L.E., The Invaders, Judd for the Defense, The Name of the Game, Bracken's World, Banyon, Harry O, Mannix, Barnaby Jones,* and *Happy Days*. She was awarded a posthumous Emmy for her work in the 1976 television movie *The Boy in the Plastic Bubble*. Her last role was as Joan Bradford in the ABC series *Eight Is Enough*.

Joyce Jillson *(Jill Smith)*

Joyce Jillson grew up in Rhode Island and made her Broadway debut in *The Roar of the Greasepaint, the Smell of the Crowd*. She first appeared on TV in *The Man from U.N.C.L.E.* Prior to being cast in *Peyton Place*. She later became the author of a nationally syndicated astrology column.

Her television work includes: *The Misadventures of Sheriff Lobo, B.J. and the Bear, The Eddie Capra Mysteries, Murder in Peyton Place* (as Jill Harrington), *Lou Grant, Kolchak: The Night Stalker, Police Woman* and *Columbo*.

John Kellogg *(Jack Chandler)*

John Kellogg began his career in New England summer stock then appeared on Broadway. He first acted in films in the 1940s, the segued into television by the early 1950s.

His filmography includes: *Orphans, Violets Are Blue, Edge of the City, The Silver Whip, The Raiders, Come Fill the Cup, The Enforcer, Kansas Raiders, Twelve O'Clock High, Port of New York,*

Station West, Sinister Journey, King of the Wild Horses, Johnny O'Clock and *A Walk in the Sun*.

His many TV credits include: *Wiseguy, St. Elsewhere, Blind Justice, Kent State, Police Story, Alias Smith and Jones, The Bold Ones: The Lawyers, Daniel Boone, Gunsmoke, The Virginian, Lancer, Bonanza, The Wild Wild West, The Invaders, Judd for the Defense, The Doomsday Flight, The Fugitive, The Outer Limits, The Great Adventure, Rawhide, The Dakotas, The Untouchables, Surfside 6, Lawman, Maverick, Hawaiian Eye,* and *Tightrope.*

John Kerr *(D.A. John Fowler)*

John Kerr began his career as an apprentice in summer stock. He was a member of the Brattle Theatre Company during his undergraduate years at Harvard. He made his Broadway debut in 1952 in *Bernardine*. In 1953, he won the Antionette Perry Award, The New York Drama Critics Award and the Donaldson Award for his sensitive portrayal of Tom Robinson Lee in *Tea and Sympathy*, a role he repeated in the 1956 feature film version (opposite Deborah Kerr). He also starred in *Gaby* (with Leslie Caron), *The Vintage* (with Pier Angel and Michele Morgan), as Lt. Joe Cable in the 1958 film version of *South Pacific*, and in the Edgar Allan Poe classic *The Pit and the Pendulum* (with Vincent Price). Kerr later appeared in many network television shows throughout the 1960s and 1970s, and also became a practicing, civil trial attorney. Ironically, he played the recurring role of prosecutor Jerry O'Brien in *The Streets of San Francisco* from 1973–1977.

A sampling of his television work includes: *Washington: Behind Closed Doors, McMillan & Wife, Police Story, Barnaby Jones, The Mod Squad, Alias Smith and Jones, The Rookies, Columbo, Dr. Simon Locke, Yuma, The Young Lawyers, The F.B.I., The Name of the Game, The High Chaparral, Run for Your Life, Twelve O'Clock High, The Long Hot Summer, Profiles in Courage, Arrest and Trial, Wagon Train, Bus Stop, Gunsmoke, Checkmate* and *Rawhide*.

Irvin Kershner (Director)

Irvin Kershner's background is a mixture of music and art. Born and raised in Philadelphia, he attended Temple University's Tyler School of Fine Art, and later studied photography at the Art Center College of Design in California. He began his film career at USC-School of Cinema teaching photography and taking cinema courses. He later worked as a director and cinematographer of documentaries in Iran, Greece and Turkey for the U.S. Information Service.

Upon his return to the U.S., he co-developed (with Paul Coates) the Emmy Award-winning *Confidential File*, a documentary TV series. Kershner later developed *The Rebel* television series, as well as the pilots for *Peyton Place*, *Cain's Hundred*, and *Philip Marlowe*.

Some of his best known feature films include: *The Hoodlum Priest, The Luck of Ginger Coffey, A Fine Madness, The Flim Flam Man, Up the Sandbox, Return of a Man Called Horse, The Eyes of Laura Mars, The Empire Strikes Back* (the second film in the *Star Wars* trilogy and one of the top one-hundred highest grossing films of all time), *Never Say Never Again* (which marked the return of Sean Connery to the role of James Bond), and *Robocop 2*.

Kershner's later television work includes the critically acclaimed *Raid on Entebbe*, (which received nine Emmy nominations including one for Best Director) and the HBO film *Traveling Man* (for which he received an ACE Award nomination.)

For many years, Kershner lectured at universities and film festivals throughout the country.

Gail Kobe (Doris Shuster)

Gail Kobe began her career as an actress and later became a producer of several daytime dramas. She appeared in network television series from the late 1950s through the early 1970s, then worked behind the camera as a supervising producer on

The Edge of Night. She later became the executive producer of *Texas* and *The Guiding Light*. She last worked as the producer of *The Bold and the Beautiful*.

Her many television appearances include: *The Legend of Lizzie Borden, Mannix, Young Dr. Kildare, Bright Promise, Daniel Boone, Bewitched, Ironside, Felony Squad, Cimarron Strip, Hogan's Heroes, A Man Called Shenandoah, The Wackiest Ship in the Army, The Outer Limits, Ben Casey, The Twilight Zone, Perry Mason, 77 Sunset Strip, The Fugitive, The Untouchables, Combat, Laramie, Empire, The Rebel, Tales of Wells Fargo, Bourbon Street Beat, Wagon Train,* and *Rescue 8*.

Paul Langton *(Leslie Harrington)*

Paul Langton first appeared on screen in the early 1940s. One of his earliest film roles was as Captain "Sky" York in *Thirty Seconds Over Tokyo*. He also appeared in *They Were Expendable, Courage of Lassie, The Sea of Grass,* and *A Star is Born*. With the advent of television, Langton appeared in several hundred programs throughout the 1950s and 1960s in addition to his continuing role on *Peyton Place*. His career continued until the early 1970s.

His many television credits include: *Emergency, My Three Sons, Ironside, The Immortal, It Takes a Thief, The Outcasts, The Travels of Jamie McPheeters, The Fugitive, The Twilight Zone, Dr. Kildare, Leave It to Beaver, Mister Ed, The Untouchable, The Eleventh Hour, Perry Mason, Wagon Train, Bus Stop, 77 Sunset Strip, Cheyenne, Gunsmoke, Adventures in Paradise, Lassie, National Velvet, Bat Masterson, Law of the Plainsman, Tales of Wells Fargo, Hawaiian Eye, Tightrope, Men into Space, The Millionaire,* and *Zane Grey Theater*.

Rita Lakin *(Staff Writer 1965–1966)*

Rita Lakin began her career as a writer on *Dr. Kildare*. In the mid 1960s, she joined the writing staff on *Peyton Place*. During the course of her career she created the ABC series *The Rookies*, developed and produced the CBS series *Flamingo Road*, and created/produced *Nightingales* on NBC.

Her television movie credits include: *Peyton Place: The Next Generation, Torn Between Two Lovers, A Sensitive, Passionate Man, Hey, I'm Alive, Message to My Daughter, A Summer Without Boys, Death Takes a Holiday,* and *Women in Chains*. Her mini-series include: *Voice of the Heart,* and *Strong Medicine*. Her episodic TV work includes: *Dynasty, Emerald Point NAS, Medical Center, The Mod Squad, Family Affair, The Invaders, Run for Your Life, The Virginian,* and *Daniel Boone*.

Dorothy Malone *(Constance MacKenzie)*

Dorothy Malone won an Academy Award (Best Actress in a Supporting Role) for her portrayal of Marylee Hadley in *Written on the Wind* (1956). She began her film career in the mid 1940s, and reached her peak in the mid to late 1950s as Diana Barrymore in *Too Much Too Soon;* as Cleva Chaney in *Man of a Thousand Faces;* as LaVerne Shumann in *The Tarnished Angels;* and as Lily Dollar in the western *Warlock*.

She became a household name from her portrayal of Constance MacKenzie on *Peyton Place;* and later played the featured role of Irene Goodwin in *Rich Man, Poor Man*. She reprised the role of Constance MacKenzie in two television movies, and made her final appearance in the feature film *Basic Instinct*.

Her filmography includes: *The Being, Winter Kills, Good Luck, Miss Wyckoff, Golden Rendezvous, Fate Is the Hunter, The Last Sunset, The Last Voyage, Pillars of the Sky, Tension at Table Rock, Sincerely Yours, The Fast and the Furious, Battle Cry, Young at Heart, The Lone Gun, Jack Slade, Torpedo Alley, Convicted, The Nevadan, Colorado Territory, South of St. Louis, The Big Sleep,* and *Night and Day*.

Her TV guest appearances include: *Matt Houston, Vega$, Flying High, The Streets of San Francisco, Police Woman, Ellery*

Queen, The November Plan, Ironside, The Bold Ones: The New Doctors, Arrest and Trial, The Untouchables, General Electric Theater, The Dick Powell Show, and *Route 66.*

Ann Marcus *(Staff Writer 1966–1969)*

Ann Marcus began her career with the *New York Daily News* and later worked for *Life* magazine. She enjoyed a lengthy, successful career as a television writer and wrote for a variety of series. After working as a staff writer on *Peyton Place* Marcus became the head writer of the daytime drama *Love is a Many Splendored Thing* followed by *Search for Tomorrow.*

In the mid 1970s, she co-created and was head writer for *Mary Hartman, Mary Hartman,* winning an Emmy in 1976. She also co-created *Fernwood 2-Nite, All That Glitters,* and *Julie Farr MD.*

Her TV movie credits include: *Women at West Point, Having Babies II,* and *Letters from Three Lovers.* She was also supervising producer of *Falcon Crest, Knots Landing* and co-wrote the miniseries *Knots Landing: Back to the Cul-de-Sac.* In 1999, she published her memoir *Whistling Girl.*

Her husband was Ellis Marcus, the successful TV writer.

George Macready *(Martin Peyton)*

George Macready was born in Providence, Rhode Island and worked as a newspaper reporter before becoming an actor. He was an accomplished Broadway performer before entering films in the early 1940s. His raspy voice and facial scar made him an ideal villain. He began to do television in the early 1950s and made several hundred appearances.

His more notable films include: *Tora! Tora! Tora!, The Great Race, Where Love Has Gone, Seven Days in May, Dead Ringer, Taras Bulba, Two Weeks in Another Town, Paths of Glory, A Kiss Before Dying, Julius Caesar, Detective Story, The Desert Fox, Knock* on *Any Door, The Big Clock, Down to Earth, Gilda, The Seventh Cross,* and *Commandos Strike at Dawn.*

His television work includes: *Daughter of the Mind, Lancer, Night Gallery, The Young Lawyers, Get Smart, The Man from U.N.C.L.E., Name of the Game, Profiles in Courage, Kentucky Jones, The Outer Limits, The Great Adventure, The Twilight Zone, Perry Mason, The Tall Man, Ripcord, The Dick Powell Show, Laramie, Adventures in Paradise, Thriller, The Rebel, Playhouse 90, The Rifleman, Riverboat, Tightrope, Bonanza, Wanted: Dead or Alive, Gunsmoke,* and *Schlitz Playhouse of Stars.*

Paul Monash *(Executive Producer)*

Paul Monash was born in Harlem, raised in the Bronx, schooled at the University of Wisconsin (B.A.) and refined at Columbia University (M.A.) As a young man, he traveled across America, served in the Merchant Marine, lived in Paris and wrote two novels. Monash accepted an invitation to write for the series *Foreign Intrigue* (filmed in Sweden) which opened up the gates of television. After writing for *Playhouse 90* and *Climax*, he won an Emmy for "The Lonely Wizard" episode of *Schlitz Playhouse of Stars*. In 1959, Monash wrote the two part episode of "The Untouchables" which aired on *Desilu Playhouse* and spawned the series. From 1961–1962 he created and was the executive producer of the NBC series *Cain's Hundred* which starred Peter Mark Richman. In the late 1960s, Monash created and executive produced *Judd, for the Defense* which starred Carl Betz and Stephen Young.

Monash's film production credits include *Butch Cassidy and the Sundance Kid* (1969), *Slaughterhouse-Five* (1972), *The Front Page* (1974), *Carrie* (1976), and *The Friends of Eddie Coyle* (which he produced and adapted for the screen).

Monash wrote the 1979 CBS-TV adaptation of *All Quiet on the Western Front*, which won a Golden Globe Award. His screenplay for *Stalin* (a 1992 HBO film) was nominated for an Emmy Award; and Monash received the Humanitas Prize for his teleplay for the TNT film *George Wallace*.

In March of 2000 the Writers Guild of America presented Monash with the Paddy Chayefsky Award for Lifetime Achievement (the guild's highest award given to writers who have advanced the literature of television through the years).

Patricia Morrow *(Rita Jacks Harrington)*

Californian Patricia Morrow began her career as a child actress in 1950s films such as *Ma and Pa Kettle at Home*, *Artists and Models*, *The Bad Seed*, and *The Wrong Man*. In the 1960s, she appeared on television in *Going My Way*, *Leave It to Beaver*, *My Three Sons*, *Perry Mason*, *Mr. Novak*, and *The Virginian* before joining the cast of *Peyton Place*. She reprised her role in the daytime drama *Return to Peyton Place* (1972–1974) and in the TV movie *Peyton Place: The Next Generation* (1985).

In the mid 1970s, she became a practicing attorney.

Leslie Nielsen *(Dr. Vincent Markham/Kenneth Markham)*

Canadian-born Leslie Nielsen has played a wide variety of comical and dramatic roles in movies and television. Younger audiences know him for his portrayal of Detective Frank Drebin in the two *Naked Gun* films and as President Harris in the *Scary Movie* series. Nielsen has appeared in over 100 films and well over 1000 television shows in his lengthy career.

A partial filmography includes: *An American Carol, Superhero Movie, Music Within, Wrongfully Accused, Mr. Magoo, Dracula: Dead and Loving It, Repossessed, Wrong is Right, Airplane, City on Fire, The Kentucky Fried Movie, Viva Knievel, The Poseidon Adventure, How to Commit Marriage, The Reluctant Astronaut, Harlow, The Sheepman, Tammy and the Bachelor, The Opposite Sex, The Vagabond King,* and *Forbidden Planet*.

His numerous TV credits include: *Santa Who?, Due South, The Golden Girls, Murder. She Wrote, Police Squad!, Backstairs* *at the White House, Kung Fu, Cannon, Streets of San Francisco, M*A*S*H, Columbo, Hawaii Five-O, The Bold Ones: The Protectors* (as Deputy Police Chief Sam Danforth), *The Virginian, The New Breed* (as Lt. Price Adams), and *The Swamp Fox* (as Colonel Francis Marion).

Ed Nelson *(Dr. Michael Rossi)*

A devoted family man and father of six children and fourteen grandchildren, Ed Nelson began his career in early 1950s New Orleans, at the NBC TV affiliate WDSU. He acted in a weekly series of live dramatic scenes *(Tulane Close-Up)* and later worked at the station as a floor director, cameraman, and played Cosmo, the host of a popular children's show that showed films and space cartoons. While employed at WDSU, Nelson was able to act in feature films being shot in the New Orleans area. He appeared in *Nightmare* starring Edward G. Robinson, and in *Steel Trap* with Joseph Cotton and Teresa Wright. Soon after working on the Roger Corman *Swamp Women*, he moved to California and began an association with Corman. Nelson appeared in twelve Corman films over a three year period (including the title role in *Attack of the Crab Monster*).

His early television career featured many guest star roles in series such as *Highway Patrol, Tightrope, Johnny Ringo, Riverboat, The Life and Legend of Wyatt Earp, M Squad, Tombstone Territory, The Deputy, The Rebel, Surfside 6, Have Gun–Will Travel, Thriller, Hennesey, Maverick, 87th Precinct, Rawhide, The Virginian, The Twilight Zone, Laramie, The Untouchables, Combat, Wagon Train, The Fugitive,* and *Arrest and Trial.* From 1964–1969, Nelson portrayed Dr. Michael Rossi, and reprised his role in two television movies: *Murder in Peyton Place* (1977) and *Peyton Place: The Next Generation* (1985).

After *Peyton Place* ended, he starred in a second TV series *The Silent Force,* and hosted *The Ed Nelson Show* (a popular morning edition) that aired for three years on the ABC TV station in Lost Angeles. Nelson continued to guest on many network series and occasionally appeared in feature films such as *Airport 1975, Midway,* and *For the Love of Benji.* In the 1980s, he portrayed Senator Mark Denning in the CBS daytime drama *Capitol.*

In the late 1990s, he returned to complete his degree at Tulane University and later taught acting and screenwriting at two local universities. In a career that spanned fifty years, Nelson appeared in forty films, over 1500 TV productions and thirty major stage productions. His autobiography *Beyond Peyton Place* was published in 2008.

Tim O'Connor *(Elliot Carson)*

Tim O'Connor attended DePaul University in Chicago (after serving in the military) intending to become an attorney. A change of heart led him to enroll at the Goodman Memorial Theatre where he studied drama and received a scholarship. After graduating, O'Connor joined the Tenthouse Theatre, a summer and winter stock company, as their resident juvenile actor performing in Highland Park, Illinois and Palm Springs, California. In New York, O'Connor first worked with a Shakespearean company off Broadway then began to appear on Broadway and in live television drama. He appeared as Jabez Stone in *The Devil and Daniel Webster* opposite Edward G. Robinson and David Wayne on NBC and in *The Gringo* with Laurence Olivier. When television production moved to California, O'Connor commuted for several years then moved west when cast as Elliot Carson in *Peyton Place* (1965–1968). He would continue to work steadily in network television for the next thirty years. Along the way, he reprised the role of Elliot Carson in the two *Peyton Place* TV movies filmed in 1977 and 1985. He also co-starred as Dr. Elias Huer in *Buck Rogers in the 25th Century* on NBC.

His numerous TV credits include: *The Burning Zone, Walker, Texas Ranger, General Hospital* (as Jack Boland), *Star Trek: The Next Generation, Grass Roots, Doogie Howser M.D., Father Dowling Mysteries, Dallas, Murder She Wrote, T.J. Hooker,*

Hardcastle and McCormack, The A-Team, Knight Rider, Matt Houston, Dynasty (as Thomas Crayford), *The Golden Gate Murders, Barnaby Jones, Kaz, Wonder Woman, Wheels, Police Woman, Lou Grant, The Streets of San Francisco, Columbo, Maude, Cannon, Matt Helm, Police Story, Phyllis, The Six Million Dollar Man, Ellery Queen, The Rockford Files, Nakia, Medical Center, The Manhunter, Banacek, The F.B.I., Gunsmoke, Banyon, Hawaii Fire-O, Longstreet, Mannix, Dan August, Daniel Boone, Lancer, House on Greenapple Road, The Name of the Game, Bracken's World, Judd for the Defense, 12 O'Clock High, The Outer Limits, East Side/West Side, The Nurses,* and *The Twilight Zone.*

Ryan O'Neal *(Rodney Harrington)*

A one-time Golden Gloves contender, Ryan O'Neal spent part of his formative years in Germany where he attended school. His acting career began in the early 1960s, when he appeared in television shows such as *The Many Loves of Dobie Gillis, The Untouchables, General Electric Theater, Bachelor Father,* and *Leave It to Beaver.* From 1962–63, he portrayed Tal Garrett in the NBC TV series *Empire* which starred Richard Egan. Following appearances in *The Virginian, Perry Mason,* and *Wagon Train,* O'Neal was cast as Rodney Harrington in *Peyton Place* and zoomed to TV stardom.

In 1970, he earned an Academy Award nomination for Best Actor in the feature film *Love Story,* and shortly after became a major film star. Over the next two decades his films include: *Wild Rovers, What's Up Doc?, The Thief Who Came to Diner, Paper Moon, Barry Lyndon, Nickelodeon, A Bridge Too Far, The Driver, Oliver's Story, The Main Event, Green Ice, So Fine, Partners, Irreconcilable Differences, Fever Pitch, Tough Guys Don't Dance,* and *Chances Are.*

In the 1990s, O'Neal returned to television and co-starred opposite Farrah Fawcett in the CBS series *Good Sports.* During the 2000–2001 season, he appeared in the TNT series *Bull,* and two years later as Jerry Fox in the NBC series *Miss Match.*

More recently, he has been seen in the Fox series *Bones* as Max Keenan and in *90210* as Spence Montgomery.

Stephen Oliver *(Lee Webber)*

After portraying menacing/abusive Lee Webber for two seasons on *Peyton Place*, Stephen Oliver co-starred as Tom Hudson in *Bracken's World*. Throughout the 1970s he guest-starred on series such as *The Immortal, The Streets of San Francisco, Code R, ChiPs,* and *Starsky and Hutch*. He also appeared as Gentleman Jim Corbett in the Steve McQueen feature *Tom Horn* and opposite Rita Hayworth in her last film *The Naked Zoo*. His other filmwork includes *The Phoenix Report, Assignment: Survive, Malibu Beach* and *The Van*. He later retired from acting in the 1990s to write screenplays.

Susan Oliver *(Ann Howard)*

Born in New York City, Susan Oliver trained at the Neighborhood Playhouse, and first appeared in live television dramas in the mid–1950s. She made her Broadway debut in 1958, and won a Tony Award for "Best Newcomer." Soon after, she went to Hollywood and appeared in countless television shows over the next three decades. In the early 1980s, she directed episodes of *M*A*S*H* and *Trapper John, M.D.*

Oliver was also a licensed pilot and attempted to become the first woman to fly a single-engine place from New York to Moscow.

Her network TV appearances include: *Freddy's Nightmares, Simon & Simon, Murder She Wrote, International Airport, Magnum P.I., Tomorrow's Child, The Love Boat, The Streets of San Francisco, Amelia Earhart, Days of Our Lives, The Manhunter Police Story, Petrocelli, Barnaby Jones, Love Story, The Magician, The F.B.I., Ghost Story, Cannon, Gunsmoke, Medical Center, The Smith Family, Night Gallery, Sarge, Longstreet, The D.A., Love American Style,*

Alias Smith and Jones, Dan August, The Name of the Game, The Virginian, Mannix, The Big Valley, The Outsider, A Man Called Gannon, The Wild Wild West, T.H.E. Cat, Tarzan, My Three Sons, Star Trek, Peyton Place (as Ann Howard), *I Spy, Gomer Pyle U.S.M.C., A Man Called Shenandoah, Dr. Kildare, The Man from U.N.C.L.E., Ben Casey, The Rogues, Destry, The Defenders, The Travels of Jamie McPheeters, The Andy Griffith Show, Burke's Law, The Fugitive, The Nurses,* 77 *Sunset Strip, Route* 66, *The Dick Powell Show, Wagon Train, Rawhide, The Alfred Hitchcock Hour, Checkmate, Cain's Hundred, Laramie, The Adventures of Ozzie and Harriet, Adventures in Paradise, Zane Grey Theater, Naked City, Michael Shayne, The Aquanauts, The Untouchables, Thriller, Wanted: Dead or Alive, The Twilight Zone, Playhouse 90, Bonanza, The Lineup, The Millionaire, Father Knows Best, Climax, The United States Steel Hour,* and *Studio One.*

Her film credits include: *Hardly Working, Ginger in the Morning, The Monitors, Change of Mind, The Love-Ins, The Disorderly Orderly, Your Cheatin' Heart, Looking for Love, Guns of Diablo, The Caretakers, Butterfield 8,* and *The Gene Krupa Story.*

Barbara Parkins *(Betty Anderson)*

Barbara Parkins was born in Vancouver, British Columbia and arrived in Hollywood while still in her teens. She studied acting, voice, and trained in ballet prior to her professional debut as an actress. In the early 1960s, she began to appear in various network TV series, and in 1964 was cast as Betty Anderson in *Peyton Place*. She remained with the series for its entire five year run. In 1966, Parkins was nominated for an Emmy Award (Best Actress in a Lead Role in a Drama Series). In 1968, she starred as Ann Welles in *Valley of the Dolls*. After *Peyton Place* ended its run, Parkins moved to England and appeared on the BBC in period dramas. She later became an accomplished photographer.

Her filmography includes: *The Kremlin Letter, The Mephisto Waltz, Puppet on a Chain, Asylum, Christina, Shout at the Devil, Bear Island,* and *Breakfast in Paris.*

Her television mini-series include: *Captains and Kings, Testimony of Two Men, The Manions of America,* and *Jennie: Lady Randolph Churchill.* Television movies: *Young Joe, the Forgotten Kennedy, Ziegfeld: The Man and His Women* (as Anna Held), *The Critical List, The Calendar Girl Murders,* and *Peyton Place: The Next Generation.*

Ted Post *(Director)*

Born in Brooklyn, Ted first studied acting with famed acting teacher Tamara Daykarhanova (from the Moscow Art Theatre), then was given a director's scholarship to the New School for Social Research Dramatic Workshop in Manhattan. Following his study, Post was signed to direct ten plays at the Cedarhurst Summer Theatre (Long Island). As a member of the 235th Engineer Combat Battalion in Italy during WWII, Post produced and directed a musical revue entitled *Bypass to Berlin* that was an outstanding success and reached 62,000 troops including the British.

After the war, Post began doing numerous summer stock productions, directing everyone from Buster Keaton in *Three Men on a Horse* to Bela Lugosi in *Dracula*.

In the 1950s, Post moved into the arena of television and over the next thirty-six years directed over 700 television shows. His feature films included directing such stars as Clint Eastwood, Burt Lancaster, Charlton Heston, Helen Hayes, and Myrna Loy. Post is a three-time nominee for Best Director of the Year by the Directors Guild of America and two-time recipient of the Western Heritage Award for Directing. He has also been an Adjunct Professor at UCLA, USC, UC–Berkeley and Claremont College.

His films include: *4 Faces, The Human Shield, Nightkill, Good Guys Wear Black, Go Tell the Spartans, Whiffs, Magnum Force, The Harrad Experiment, Beneath the Planet of the Apes,* and *Hang 'em High.*

His many television credits include: *Cagney and Lacey,*

Beyond Westworld, Columbo, Baretta, Monty Nash, Five Desperate Women, Yuma, Dr. Cook's Garden, Bracken's World, The Twilight Zone, Combat, Suspense, Rawhide, Gunsmoke, The Defenders, The Virginian, Empire, Thriller, Wagon Train, Bus Stop, The Detectives, General Electric Theater, Follow the Sun, Laramie, Checkmate, Route 66, The Rifleman, Tombstone Territory, Perry Mason, Zane Grey Theater, West Point, Medic, Waterfront, Schlitz Playhouse of Stars, and *Armstrong Circle Theatre.*

Don Quine *(Joe Chernak)*

Don Quine is best remembered by *Peyton Place* fans as the troublemaking Joe Chernak. He also portrayed Stacy Grainger on *The Virginian* for two seasons (1966–1968). His network television credits include: *Hawaii Five-O, U.M.C.* (the pilot film for Medical Center), *Lancer, Insight, The F.B.I., 12 O'Clock High, The Fugitive, Dr. Kildare, Rawhide,* and *The Detectives Starring Robert Taylor.*

Del Reisman *(Story Editor/Associate Producer 1965–1969)*

Del Reisman began his career in the days of live television in the 1950s. He worked on such shows as *NBC Matinee Theater,* and then as story editor for the acclaimed *Playhouse 90,* working with producer Martin Manulis, writers Rod Serling, David Shaw, Robert Alan Arthur, as well as directors John Frankenheimer, Franklin Schaffner, George Roy Hill, Arthur Penn, and Arthur Hiller. Reisman went on to become story editor for *The Twilight Zone,* then produced, wrote or edited episodes of *The Untouchables, Rawhide, Peyton Place, The Streets of San Francisco, Cannon, The Blue Knight, Banacek, Cagney and Lacey,* and *The Yellow Rose* among many others.

Reisman served as President of the Writers Guild of America West (1991–1993) as well as the WGAW's Vice President (1987–1991), and was a member of WGAW Board of Directors (1979–1987). He also chaired three consecutive

WGAW negotiating committees, and served as chairman or member of twenty other Guild committees. He is a member of the Board of Trustees, Writers Guild Federation. In addition, he is a member of the faculty at the American Film Institute teaching screenwriting, and is a Member of the National Film Preservation Board, Library of Congress.

During World War II, as a member of the USAF, Reisman completed a tour of duty that included thirty-five missions over Germany.

Percy Rodriguez *(Dr. Harry Miles)*

Percy Rodriguez was born in Montreal, Canada of Afro-Portuguese heritage. He made his Broadway debut in Lillian Hellman's *Toy in the Attic* in 1960. With a deep, authoritative voice and articulate manner, he often played intelligent men of authority. After his retirement from acting, he continued to provide narrations and voiceovers.

His television appearances include: *Perry Mason: The Case of the Sinister Spirit, Benson, The Atlanta Child Murders, This Girl for Hire, Shadow of Death, T.J. Hooker, Dynasty, The Fall Guy, Sanford, The Night Rider, The Duke, Roots: The Next Generations, Ring of Passion, The Jeffersons, The Hardy Boys/Nancy Drew Mysteries, Gemini Man, Executive Suite, Most Wanted, Medical Center, The Lives of Jenny Dolan, Planet of the Apes, Apple's Way, Toma, Shaft, Genesis 11, The Rookies, Sixth Sense, Banacek, Cannon, The Forgotten Man, The Name of the Game, Mission: Impossible, Mannix, Then Came Bronson, Marcus Welby M.D., Tarzan, The Fugitive, Star Trek, The Wild Wild West, Ben Casey, Route 66, The Nurses,* and *Naked City.*

Kasey Rogers *(Julie Anderson)*

Kasey Rogers was given the nickname "Casey" by grade school classmates impressed by her ability to hit a baseball further than almost anyone else. (She later changed the "C" in her name to a "K".) She was placed under contract to Paramount in her early twenties, in 1949, and appeared briefly in films such as *Chicago Deadline, Samson and Delilah, Union Station,* and *A Place in the Sun.* Billed by the studio as Laura Elliot, she then appeared in *Strangers on a Train, Two Lost Worlds, Silver City, Jamaica Run, The French Line,* and *About Mrs. Leslie.*

In the mid 1950s, she began to do television and soon after, changer her name back after leaving Paramount. She worked consistently in shows such as *The Millionaire, Sergeant Preston of the Yukon, Richard Diamond, Private Detective, The Restless Gun, M-Squad, Lawman, Cheyenne, Hennesey, Perry Mason, Maverick, Thriller,* and *The Lucy Show,* prior to being cast in *Peyton Place.* From 1966–1972, she appeared as Louise Tate on *Bewitched.*

Her additional TV credits include: *The Invisible Man, Marcus Welby M.D., Lucas Tanner, Longstreet, Adam-12, The Bold Ones: The New Doctors,* and *Mission Impossible.*

Gena Rowlands *(Adrienne Van Leyden)*

Gena Rowlands (a three-time Emmy Award winner) first attended the University of Wisconsin, then left for New York where she studied drama at the American Academy of Dramatic Art. On stage, she went from understudy to lead role in the original Broadway production of *The Seven Year Itch,* and opened in *The Middle of the Night* opposite Edward G. Robinson in 1956.

On TV, she appeared in anthology series such as *Robert Montgomery Presents, Kraft Television Theatre, Armstrong Circle Theatre, Studio One,* and *The U.S. Steel Hour.* She made her film debut in *The High Cost of Loving* with Jose Ferrer in 1958. In 1961, she co-starred on NBC's *87th Precinct.*

Teaming with husband writer/director John Cassavetes, she co-starred in *A Child is Waiting* (with Judy Garland and Burt Lancaster), *Faces, Gloria* (nominated for Academy Award for Best Actress), *Love Streams, Minnie and Moskowitz, She's So Lovely,* and *A Woman Under the Influence* (Academy Award nomination).

In recent years, Rowlands has starred in *The Notebook* (opposite James Garner) which was directed by her son, Nick Cassavetes; and in 2008, she appeared in the film *Broken English*, written and directed by daughter Zoe Cassavetes.

Her filmography includes: *The Skeleton Key, Taking Lives, The Weekend, The Mighty, Hope Floats, Paulie, She's So Lovely, Unhook the Stars, The Neon Bible, Something to Talk About, Silent Cries, Night on Earth, Once Around, Another Woman, Light of Day, Tempest,* and *Two-Minute Warning*.

Her many television credits include: *NCIS, Monk, What if God Were the Sun?, The Incredible Mrs. Ritchie* (Emmy Award winner), *Hysterical Blindness* (Emmy Award winner), *Wild Iris, The Color of Love: Jacey's Story, Best Friends for Life, Parallel Lives, Crazy in Love, Montana, The Betty Ford Story, An Early Frost, Strangers: The Story of a Mother and Daughter, A Question of Love, Columbo, Medical Center,* and *Ghost Story*.

Barbara Rush *(Marsha Russell)*

Originally from Denver, Colorado, Barbara Rush got her start at the Pasadena Playhouse then signed with Paramount Pictures. She made her screen debut in the 1951 movie *The Goldbergs*. In 1954, she won a Golden Globe Award for her performance in *It Came from Outer Space*.

Her notable films throughout the 1950s and 1960s include: *Magnificent Obsession, Bigger Than Life, Harry Black and the Tiger, The Young Lions, The Young Philadelphians, The Bramble Bush, Strangers When We Meet, Come Blow Your Horn, Robin and the Seven Hoods,* and *Hombre*.

In the 1960s and 1970s, she appeared more frequently on television guesting in *Ben Casey, The Outer Limits, Convoy, Dr. Kildare, The Fugitive, Laredo, Batman, Love American Style, The Mod Squad, Night Gallery, Marcus Welby M.D., McCloud, Ironside, The Streets of San Francisco, Medical Center, Police Story, Mannix, Ellery Queen, The Bionic Woman,* and *The Love Boat*. In the 1980s, she appeared as Eudora Weldon in *Flamingo Road*, and guest starred in *Matt Houston, Fantasy Island, Finders of Lost Loves, Hotel, Magnum P.I., Murder She Wrote,* and *Hooperman.* In the 1990s, she portrayed Nola Orsini on *All My Children.* More recently she played the recurring role of Ruth Camden in the long running series *7th Heaven.*

Evelyn Scott *(Ada Jacks)*

Evelyn grew up in New England and eventually moved to Los Angeles. She began her career as a disc jockey on radio station KMPC's morning show. In the 1950s, she began to appear in network television shows as well as several feature films. She reprised the role of Ada Jacks on the NBC daytime drama *Return to Peyton Place* (1972–1974) and *Peyton Place: The Next Generation* (1985).

Her film credits include: *I Want to Live, The Green-Eyed Blond, Back From the Dead,* and *Wicked Woman.*

Her television work includes: *Channing, Bonanza, Bachelor Father, The Untouchables, Mike Hammer, M Squad, Perry Mason, The Loretta Young Show, The Restless Gun, Navy Log, Code 3, Dragnet, Make Room for Daddy, Gunsmoke, Strange Stories, Big Town, The Lone Wolf, Treasury Men in Action, I Married Joan,* and *Schlitz Playhouse of Stars.*

William Self *(Executive in charge of TV Production)*

William Self began his theatrical career as an actor appearing in over thirty films including such classics as *Monsieur Verdoux, Red River, The Great Gatsby, Battleground, Adam's Rib, Sands of Iwo Jima, Operation Pacific, The Thing from Another World,* and *Pat and Mike.*

He began his career behind the camera as a production assistant on the *China Smith* TV series and eventually became the producer of *Schlitz Playhouse of Stars.* He later produced *The Frank Sinatra Show* on ABC, then was hired by CBS as a production executive where he produced the pilot for *The Twilight Zone*. In 1959, he moved to 20th Century Fox as an executive producer. After developing the series *Hong Kong* (starring Rod Taylor) (1960–1961), Self became executive producer of *Adventures in Paradise* during seasons two and three (1960–1962).

Over a period of fifteen years, Self was promoted to Vice President in Charge of TV Production, to President of 20th Century Fox Television. In 1975, he joined Mike Frankovich in forming Frankovich/Self Productions to produce two feature films: *The Shootist* (John Wayne's final film), and *From Noon 'til Three* (starring Charles Bronson). Self returned to CBS in 1977 as V.P., Head of the West Coast Division. Later he was named VP in Charge of Movies and Mini-series. In 1982, he became President of the CBS Theatrical Films Division. In 1985, he left CBS to form Self Productions Inc. Hallmark Hall of Fame sponsored his first production: *The Tenth Man* (starring Anthony Hopkins). Later, Self partnered with Glenn Close in forming a new production company: Sarah Productions. This company provided *Hallmark Hall of Fame* with three television movies: *Sarah, Plain and Tall*; *Skylark*; and *Winter's End*.

Jack Senter *(Art Director)*

Jack Senter began his career at Paramount as senior set designer on such films as *Samson and Delilah*, *The Greatest Show on Earth*, and *The Ten Commandments*.

His feature films (as an art director) include: *Far and Away*, *Micki & Maude*, *Go Tell the Spartans*, *Return from Witch Mountain*, *Oh, God!*, *Greased Lightning*, *Freaky Friday*, *Obsession*, *No Deposit, No Return*, and *The Strongest Man in the World*.

His television work (as an art director) includes: *Picking Up the Pieces*, *The Execution*, *The Fighter*, *Masada*, *Centennial*, *Disneyland*, *The Young Runaways*, *The Trial of Chaplain Jensen*, *Ordeal*, *M*A*S*H*, *Cade's County*, *The Forgotten Man*, *Nanny and the Professor*, *Julia*, *Gilligan's Island*, *Voyage to the Bottom of the Sea*, *The Many Loves of Dobie Gillis*, *Follow the Sun*, and *Five Fingers*.

Kent Smith *(Dr. Robert Morton)*

Kent Smith began his career on the stage and by the early 1940s was appearing in feature films. With the advent of television in the 1950s, Smith frequently appeared on shows such as *The Philco Television Playhouse, Studio One, Hallmark Hall of Fame, Robert Montgomery Presents,* and *Lux Video Theater.* His productive career continued well into the 1970s.

Feature films include: *Billy Jack Goes to Washington, Big Mo, Lost Horizon, Pete 'n' Tillie, The Games, Death of a Gunfighter, Assignment to Kill, Kona Coast, The Money Jungle, Games, A Covenant with Death, The Trouble with Angels, The Young Lovers, Youngblood Hawke, A Distant Trumpet, The Balcony, Susan Slade, Strangers When We Meet, This Earth Is Mine, The Mugger, Party Girl, The Badlanders, Imitation General, Sayonara, Comanche, Paula, This Side of the Law, The Damned Don't Cry, My Foolish Heart, The Fountainhead, The Voice of the Turtle, Magic Town, Nora Prentiss, The Spiral Staircase, The Curse of the Cat People, Three Russian Girls, This Land Is Mine, Forever and a Day, Hitler's Children, Three Cadets, Cat People,* and *The Garden Murder Case.*

His television work includes: *Wonder Woman, Gibbsville, Once an Eagle, Barnaby Jones, The Disappearance of Flight 412, The Cat Creature, The Streets of San Francisco, The Affair, Night Gallery, The Judge and Jake Wyler, Owen Marshall: Counselor at Law, The Delphi Bureau, Probe, The Night Stalker, Another Part of the Forest, The Last Child, The Governor and J.J., The F.B.I., How Awful about Allan, The Wild Wild West, Daniel Boone, Mission: Impossible, Felony Squad, The Man from U.N.C.L.E., Peyton Place* (as Dr. Robert Morton), *I Spy, A Man Called Shenandoah, The Alfred Hitchcock Hour, The Great Adventure, The Eleventh Hour, Rawhide, The Outer Limits, Arrest and Trial, The Untouchables, Going My Way, The Wide Country, Perry Mason, Have Gun–Will Travel, Cain's Hundred, 77 Sunset Strip, Checkmate, Bronco, Adventures in Paradise, The Defenders, Lawman, Wagon Train, Dan Raven, Michael Shayne, The Millionaire, Naked City,* and *The General Electric Theater.*

William Smithers *(David Schuster)*

William Smithers was born in Richmond, Virginia and had an established stage career before his foray into network television.

He made his Broadway debut at Tybalt in *Romeo and Juliet* (which starred Olivia de Havilland) winning a Theater World Award. He also received an Obie Award for his portrayal of Treplev in Chekov's *The Sea Gull*. Other Broadway plays include: *Legend or Lovers, End as a Man, The Square Root of Wonderful,* and *Man and Boy.*

He later appeared in six feature films including *Papillon, Scorpio,* and *Attack,* and nearly 400 television shows. From 2003–2005, he created, produced and directed *The Santa Barbara Theatre of the Air* for KCSB radio, broadcasting works of classic and contemporary playwrights. (Available for free download at theatre-of-the-air.com/wordpress). Smithers and his wife Lorrie Hull Smithers (author of *Strasberg's Method: As Taught by Lorrie Hull*) now co-host the Santa Barbara Channel's television interview program *Just Between Us*. (Previous broadcasts online at SB-justbetweenus.com.)

His television credits include: *Walker Texas Ranger, Hunter, Dallas* (as Jeremy Wendell), *Sledge Hammer, Scarecrow and Mrs. King, Quincy M.E., Barnaby Jones, Doctor's Private Lives, Lucan, Executive Suite* (as Anderson Galt), *Most Wanted, The Streets of San Francisco, The Manhunter, Cannon, The Six Million Dollar Man, The Rookies, Hawkins, Cade's County, The Neon Ceiling, The Name of the Game, The Brotherhood of the Bell, Ironside, Marcus Welby M.D., The Mod Squad, Hawaii Five-O, The F.B.I., The Monk, It Takes a Thief, Star Trek, Mannix, Mission: Impossible, The Invaders, Tarzan, Judd for the Defense, Felony Squad, Voyage to the Bottom of the Sea, Combat, The Defenders,* and *Studio One.*

Leigh Taylor-Young *(Rachel Welles)*

Leigh Taylor-Young has earned acclaim as an Emmy Award winning actress, as an international spokesperson for the Institute for Individual and World Peace, and as a Special Advisor in Arts and Media for the United Nations Environment Programme. Born to a diplomatic family in Washington D.C., Taylor-Young studied drama at Northwestern University (under renowned teacher Alvina Krause) and became the youngest member of the distinguished Eaglesmere Summer Repertory Theatre. In New York she continued her studies with Sanford Meisner at the Neighborhood Playhouse; and subsequently appeared on Broadway.

In addition to her accomplished stage work, Taylor-Young has appeared in numerous feature films and television series. In her first major film role she starred opposite Peter Sellers in the comedy *I Love You, Alice B. Toklas*. Some of her best-known credits include: *Jagged Edge* (with Glenn Close and Jeff Bridges), *Looker* (with Albert Finney), *Soylent Green* (with Charlton Heston), and *The Horsemen* (with Omar Sharif). Additional films include: *The Big Bounce, The Adventurers, The Buttercup Chain, The Games, The Gang That Couldn't Shoot Straight, Secret Admirer, Honeymoon Academy, Accidents, Bliss, Addams Family Reunion*, and *Slackers*.

Her television work includes regular roles in: *Peyton Place, Dallas, Picket Fences* (for which she won the Emmy), *The Devlin Connection, Hamptons, The Sentinel, Sunset Beach, Beverly Hills 90210, The Pretender,* and *Passions*. Her television movies include: *Marathon, Napoleon and Josephine, Perry Mason: The Case of the Sinister Spirit, Who Gets the Friends?, Moment of Truth: Murder or Memory?, An Unfinished Affair,* and *Stanger in My Home*.

In recent years, Taylor-Young has become an ordained minister in the Movement of Spiritual Inner Awareness and works closely with John Roger, an educator and wayshower.

Glynn Turman *(Lew Miles)*

Glynn Turman has enjoyed a career as an actor, writer, director and producer. Born in New York City, he first appeared on Broadway at age twelve as Travis Younger in Lorraine Hansberry's *A Raisin in the Sun*. A graduate of Manhattan's

School of Performing Arts, Turman apprenticed in regional theaters including the Tyrone Guthrie Repertory Theatre. He later won several NAACP Image Awards for his work on stage as an actor and director.

On television he directed episodes of the series *A Different World*, in which he appeared as retired Colonel Brad Taylor; and later directed segments of *The Parent 'Hood*, *Hangin' with Mr. Cooper*, and *The Wayans Bros*. In 2007 his portrayal of Mayor Clarence Royce in the HBO series *The Wire* earned him a third NAACP Image Award. In 2008, he won an Emmy Award for his guest appearance on the HBO series *In Treatment*. He later produced and performed a one man show *Movin' Man* about his life.

His filmography includes: *Kings of the Evening*, *Sahara*, *Men of Honor*, *Light It Up*, *How Stella Got Her Groove Back*, *Psalms from the Underground*, *The Inkwell*, *Deep Cover*, *Out of Bounds*, *Gremlins*, *A Hero Ain't Nothin' but a Sandwich*, *The River Niger*, *Cooley High*, *Together Brothers*, *Thomasine & Bushrod*, and *Five on the Black Hand Side*.

His television work includes: *Flash Forward*, *Southland*, *In Treatment*, *Scrubs*, *ER*, *Cold Case*, *Night Life*, *Law & Order: Special Victims Unit*, *The Bernie Mac Show*, *Law & Order: Criminal Intent*, *Resurrection Blvd.*, *JAG*, *Big Apple* (as Ted Olsen), *Touched by an Angel*, *Buffalo Soldiers*, *Someone Else's Child*, *Murder She Wrote*, *J.J. Starbuck*, *Matlock*, *The Twilight Zone*, *Riptide*, *T.J. Hooker*, *Fantasy Island*, *The Love Boat*, *Fame*, *The White Shadow*, *Attica*, *Centennial*, *The Paper Chase*, and *The Blue Knight*.

Elizabeth Walker *(Carolyn Russell)*

Elizabeth Walker was born in New York City. She made her film debut at age sixteen opposite Peter Sellers in *The World of Henry Orient*. Soon after, she appeared in multiple episodes of *Dr. Kildare*. After *Peyton Place*, Walker appeared in the television movie *Seven in Darkness*. She made two more films in the early 1970s: *The Jesus Trip* and *Jennifer on My Mind*. Her final TV appearance was in an episode of *The Sixth Sense* (1972).

Ruth Warrick *(Hannah Cord)*

Ruth Warrick was born in St. Joseph, Missouri and began her career in the 1940s as a radio singer. She made her film debut in *Citizen Kane* as Emily Monroe Norton. Her noteworthy 1940s films include: *Journey into Fear, The Corsican Brothers, Song of the South,* and *Daisy Kenyon*.

In the 1950s, she appeared first on *The Guiding Light* (as Janet Johnson R.N.) then later joined *As the World Turns* (as Edith Hughes). In the early 1960s, she starred opposite Leon Ames and Myrna Fahey in the CBS TV series *Father of the Bride*. Warrick was cast as Hannah Cord in *Peyton Place* in 1965 and received an Emmy Award nomination in 1967. That same year she made her exit; but returned briefly during the final season.

In 1970, Warrick was cast in a new daytime soap opera *All My Children* as Phoebe Tyler. She played the role for over thirty years, and received a Daytime Emmy Award for Lifetime Achievement in 2004.

John Wilder *(Staff Writer 1965–1968)*

John Wilder has written and/or produced nearly 400 hours of prime-time television drama on network and cable and been commissioned to write theatrical features by Columbia Pictures, Warner Bros., Tristar, Orion, 20th Century Fox, and Universal Pictures.

He has received the Writers Guild of America Award for Best Long-Form Teleplay, and received WGA nominations for Best Long-Form Series and Best Episodic Drama. Wilder also won the Western Writers of America Award for Best Television Film, and the Chicago International Film Festival Award for Best Television Series. He has received two TV Academy Emmy nominations for Best Dramatic Series and received Golden Globe nominations for Best Picture Made for Television, and for Best Drama Series.

He had the honor and privilege of mounting the biggest

television event of its time, the epic twenty-six hour mini-series of James Michener's *Centennial* for NBC, adapting the best-selling novel and executive producing the series for Universal.

He worked with Larry McMurtry to write and executive produce a sequel to McMurtry's Pulitzer-Prize winning novel, creating the seven-hour mini-series: *Return to Lonesome Dove* for CBS. He adapted John Jake's best-selling novel *The Bastard* for OPT, was chosen again by James Michener to adapt his best-selling novel *Texas* for ABC; and was selected by Anne Rice to adapt her novel *The Feast of All Saints* for Showtime.

He created and executive produced two critically-acclaimed series for Warner Bros., *The Yellow Rose* (NBC) and *Spenser: For Hire* (ABC) on which he teamed with the dean of crime fiction, Robert B. Parker. Wilder also produced *The Streets of San Francisco* (ABC) for Quinn Martin.

He recently adapted Anne Rice's biggest selling novel *The Witching Hour* as a ten-hour mini-series for Warner Bros. Television and NBC; wrote an original screenplay, *The 9th Ward*, based on a true story about the heroic actions of a New Orleans police officer during Hurricane Katrina, for Universal Pictures; adapted *Island of Saints*, a novel by best-selling author Andy Andrews as an independent film, and adapted best-selling author Nicholas Evans' novel *The Smoke Jumper*, as a screenplay titled *Hearts of Fire* for Universal.

Lana Wood *(Sandy Webber)*

Lana Wood was born in Santa Monica, California, the younger sister of actress Natalie Wood. She made her screen debut as a child actress in John Ford's *The Searchers* followed by appearances in *Playhouse 90*, *The Real McCoys*, and the feature films *Marjorie Morningstar* and *Five Finger Exercise*. After appearing on 1960s series such as *Dr. Kildare*, *The Fugitive*, and *Bonanza*, Wood was placed under contract to 20th Century Fox and cast as Eula Harker in the ABC TV series *The Long Hot Summer*. After the show's cancellation, Wood joined the cast of *Peyton*

Place as Sandy Webber then guested on the TV series *My Friend Tony*, *Felony Squad*, and *The Wild Wild West*.

In the early 1970s, Wood appeared as Plenty O'Toole in the seventh Bond film, *Diamonds Are Forever*. She continued to work well into the 1980s.

Her television credits include: *Mike Hammer*, *The Fall Guy*, *Capitol* (as Fran Burke), *Nero Wolfe*, *Captain America II: Death Too Soon*, *Starsky & Hutch*, *Fantasy Island*, *Police Story*, *A Question of Guilt*, *QBVII*, *Mission: Impossible*, *Night Gallery*, *Disneyland*, *Monty Nash*, *O'Hara U.S. Treasury*, *Marcus Welby M.D.*, *The Over the Hill Gang Rides Again*, and *Black Water Gold*.

Endnotes

(Telephone and Email interviews unless otherwise noted.)

1. William Self, October 2009, California.
2. Irvin Kershner, February 2010, California.
3. John Wilder, April 2010, California.
4. Tim O'Connor, October 2009, California.
5. Ryan O'Neal, February 2010, California.
6. Everett Chambers, October 2009, California.
7. Barbara Parkins, February 2010, California.
8. Dorothy Malone, November 2009, Texas.
9. Ed Nelson, (from his book *Beyond Peyton Place*, Word Association Publishers, 2008).
10. David Canary, April 2010, Connecticut.
11. Paul Monash, (from his story/character notes, 1965).
12. Richard De Roy, (from the interview with Stephen Bowie, http://www.classictvhistory.com).
13. Lee Grant, February 2010, New York.
14. Ted Post, November 2009, California.
15. Del Reisman, December 2009, New York.
16. Rita Lakin, November 2009, California.
17. Michael Gleason, April 2010, California.
18. Leigh Taylor-Young, February 2010, California.
19. John Kerr, October 2009, California.

20. Walter Doniger, (from the article "Interviews with Directors", Westview Press, 1978)
21. Robert Hogan, November 2009, New York.
22. Jeffrey Hayden, October 2009, California.
23. John Erman, November 2009, New York.
24. Tom Del Ruth, October 2009, California.
25. Jack Senter, November 2009, California.
26. Michael Christian, November 2009, California.
27. Ruby Dee, December 2009, New York.
28. Elizabeth Walker, May 2010, Connecticut.
29. Ann Marcus, November 2009, California.

About The Author

BORN AND RAISED in Philadelphia, James Rosin graduated from Temple University's School of Communications with a degree in broadcasting. In New York he studied acting with Bobby Lewis and appeared in plays off-off Broadway, in New England summer stock, and on the ABC soap opera *Edge of Night*. In Los Angeles, Rosin played featured and co-starring roles on TV in Mickey Spillane's *Mike Hammer, T.J. Hooker, Quincy M.E., The Powers of Matthew Star, Cannon, Mannix, Banacek, Adam-12, Love American Style*, and two mini-series, *Loose Change* and *Once an Eagle*.

His film credits include: *Up Close and Personal, Sleepers,* and *The Adventures of Buckaroo Banzai*. He also wrote stories and teleplays for *Quincy M.E.* (NBC), *Capitol* (CBS), and *Loving Friends and Perfect Couples* (Showtime). His full-length play, *Michael in Beverly Hills,* a comedy-drama, premiered at American Theater Arts in Los Angeles and was later presented off-off Broadway at the American Musical Dramatic Academy's Studio One Theater.

In recent years, Rosin has written and produced two one-hour sports documentaries which have aired on public television: *Philly Hoops: The SPHAS and Warriors* (about the first two professional basketball teams in the City of Philadelphia), and *The Philadelphia Athletics 1901–1954* (about the former American League franchise), both recently released by Alpha Video. His first book, *Philly Hoops: The SPHAS and Warriors* was published in 2003, followed by *Rock, Rhythm and Blues* (2004), *Philadelphia: City of Music* (2006), *Route 66: The Television Series* (2007, revised 2011), *Naked City: The Television Series* (2008), *Wagon Train: The Television Series* (2008, revised 2011), *Adventures in Paradise: The Television Series* (2009), *Quincy M.E.: The Television Series* (2009), *The Invaders: A Quinn Martin TV Series* and *Peyton Place: The Television Series* (both in 2010), and *The Streets of San Francisco: A Quinn Martin TV Series* (2011).

He has also been a contributing writer to *Classic Images* and *Films of the Golden Age Magazine*.

A LOOK BACK at our memorable classic television series featuring commentary from show's lead actors, guest stars, episode summaries, photos, and biographies.

Here's what readers and reviewers are saying about author JAMES ROSIN's TV books...

> "His access to many of the original cast and crew gives this offering a solid credibility."

> "...series fans will enjoy the history, photos and storytelling"

> "Filled with interesting details that will please most enthusiasts of the series."

Order your copies today at: www.**classictvseriesbooks**.com